SOLVING
LIFE

Dr. Dennis L. Harper

Copyright © 2020 Dr. Dennis L. Harper

All rights are reserved under International and Pan-American Copyright Conventions. Except for brief passages quoted in a newspaper, magazine, radio or television review, no part of this book may be reproduced in any form or by any means, electronic or mechanical, including photocopying and recording, or by any information storage and retrieval system, without permission in writing from the author.

Text in Minion Pro and Times New Roman.

First Edition, 2020, manufactured in USA
1 2 3 4 5 6 7 8 9 10 CS 26 25 24 23 22 21

All stories, photographs, and author biographical details, in this edition, are reproduced by kind permission of the author.

After extensive interviews, this book was transcribed, and copy edited by Jennifer Blakeslee Peterson. Final edit by Shirley Harper

ISBN-13: 978-1-7364204-0-9 (Paperback)

This is a picture of my dad and I, above us hangs a picture of my dad and I hunting in 1979 in Eastern Oregon. This picture with him was taken six months before he died. My dad gave me my passion for the outdoors. I lived my life to hunt and fish. I found a lot of relaxation out in nature. It's ironic that my dad died on November 7. The picture below is my Moose Hunt, also taken on November 7, five years after my dad died. My dad and I spent many evenings around the campfire talking. I write about this event in the book. It was the hunt of a lifetime, a dream come true. I felt like my dad was with me. He started me on a book years ago called *Psycho Cybernetics*. It was a motivational book that I tried to read several times and never did finish. He swore it was the best book he ever read.

DEDICATIONS

To Terry Harper, my father,
and Shirley, my beloved wife.

Shirley came into my life under strange circumstances. I thought of her as the ice bitch…from hell. When I looked beyond the surface, I realized how wrong I was. She offered ME a glimpse into my own soul, which changed my life forever. I am so blessed having her in my life.

Contents

Introduction: "You don't know what you don't know"
                              —Donald Rumsfeld
by Dr. Dennis L. Harper   xi

1   "I don't know my name."—Grace VanderWaal   1

2   "Make it simple but significant."—Don Draper   8

3   "What comes easy won't last, and what lasts does not come easy."—Unknown   18

4   "Believe that tomorrow will be better than today! —Unknown   22

5   "Ideas come from everything."—Alfred Hitchcock   25

6   "Don't judge my story by the chapter you walked in on."—Unknown   32

7   "Adventure is worthwhile!"—Aesop   40

8   "Life is what happens when you're busy making other plans."—John Lennon   46

9   "It is health that is the real wealth, and not pieces of gold and silver!"—Mahatma Gandhi   58

10 "One cannot think well, love well, sleep well, if one has not dined well!"—Virginia Woolf   76

11 "Emotion is messy, contradictory, and true."
—Nigella Lawson   82

12 "Time is precious, make sure you spend it with the right people."—Unknown   88

13 "Reality is merely an illusion, albeit a real persistent one." —Albert Einstein   91

Epilogue: "…the rest of the story."—Paul Harvey   98

Prologue

Everyone keeps looking for the magic playbook that solves all your problems and deals with every circumstance of life. I think the memo is out that that does not totally exist. What I hope to accomplish in this book is to bring you to the point of asking the question: "How do I get the most out of my life?"

It is my sincere hope that when you read this book you will benefit from my journey, the experiences I had, the wrong turns I've taken and the insights I've gained. And in the end, I hope that you will be able to say with certainty, "Today is the Best Day of My life and Tomorrow will be Even Better"!

Introduction

"You don't know what you don't know"

—*Donald Rumsfeld*

What do I do? Wake up in the morning. How many times do you get up in the morning and think, "What do I have to do? What should I do?" or, "What do I need to do?" How much are we driven by what we think we need to do? What should we really be doing?

I am haunted by the conversation I had with a man on a flight about three years ago. He was phenomenally successful having a construction company that had over a thousand employees. He started work in his 20s as a carpenter, did everything on his own, and built a billion-dollar company. I told him about several ideas that I wanted to work on, everything from building a destination clinic for doctors, to building my practice, and teaching my alternative classes to doctors. He looked at me and said, "You need to focus on one thing instead of so many things." I'm exceptionally good at being a doer. If someone comes up and asks, "Can you help do this? Can you do that? Can you do some political stuff? Can you do some fundraising? Can you help with the Chamber of Commerce? Can you help with Kiwanis?" mostly, I say yes to many projects. The classic idea is that you ask a busy person to do it and he or she ends up getting the most things done. I tend to agree with that concept, other than busyness tends to then rule your life.

The challenge is making the transition back to being in control of your life, not your life being in control of you. So, let's take some steps to make this work.

My wife and I have spent weekends on Dworshak Reservoir lately. I took every Friday off in July so we could leave on Thursday nights and camp out on our boat. We have a very modest boat that accommodates all our needs, we are able to sleep, and cook on the boat. We anchor at night next to the bank and build a bonfire on the shore. It's a good time to sit and watch the sunset, and the stars come out. It is an opportunity to talk about what life will bring the next day.

It's nice to reach a point when you can take time off and not think about what you should be doing or feel guilty that you're not working on something, returning to shoulder a lot of anxiety by rules given to us by parents and society. Everything from *you need to work harder and longer* then retire, *you are not good enough* and *you don't do enough.* Or it could be that maybe you are told you goof off too much while working 60 hours every week. There is an element of balance that comes into play. It does not mean everybody needs to be a millionaire or that everybody needs to be powerful. It means you need be to genuinely happy with your life. Not just doing fun things to be happy but being *genuinely happy.*

The first thing is to recognize if you are in that loop. Am I chasing something because someone told me I should chase it? Do I truly feel happy every day? Do I wake up without feeling guilty for not doing something? Self-evaluation now is essential to going forward.

Let's get started! In so many of the books I have read, you must read to the very end to find anything of value. I want to start by giving you an outline to be able to read the rest of the book and a task to start understanding the rest of the book. If you use a remarkably simple format, it can truly make a difference.

It is important to take a piece of paper in a moment where you do not feel rushed or pushed. Simply list all the basic items you are involved in. They could be several items at work; others could be recreational activities that might rule your life more than you realize. It is amazing how that too can get out of control.

I have a friend that's overly-compulsive with any hobby he takes on. He buys all the best parts, buys all the best toys, and pushes every minute of his spare time to fill his day. It is important to ask if that's what truly makes you happy. In most cases we find it does not. It only serves to fill time and distracts us from looking at what possibly is the best activity we should be doing. Find a peaceful place and sit down with a notepad, making a list of projects you are actively involved in doing or things that take up some of your thoughts, placing importance on them. Just make a list of things that take your time and mental energy.

You must be careful about not taking on things that you have no ability to affect. There may be social events happening that include riots and demonstrations. You have to look at those items as to what you can do (or not do) to have an effect. You might be sucked into someone else's ideology that does not fit what truly makes you happy and where you can make no difference. When you look at these topics and make this list, be honest with yourself about what you can affect.

You have a certain skillset that can always be expanded, but you must find those things that you are accomplished at. If you are not a great public speaker and don't like speaking in front of a crowd, don't get into a project that involves you speaking in public settings. Years ago, I was determined to take a typing class to improve my typing skills. Someone said to me, "Why on Earth are you wasting your time typing when someone else can do it for you?" Today, I simply use voice-to-text technology and still do not type any better than I did before, but I accomplished the end goal, which was to put things on paper. Is there a project or idea you can examine closer? Consider the thoughts or process behind it.

After you make your list, break down under each of the items what time and skillsets are required. If you want to work on remodeling your house, you have to look at finances, time that you want to put into it, or what it would cost to hire someone else to complete the project.

If you want to look at having some family time, look at your availability and what really would make sense. It is easy to say, "I want to take the family to Hawaii," but it's also tough to look at spending $15,000 or $20,000 to take eight or ten people there. Maybe you could just have a barbecue at home.

Go through all these topics. You may find some of these items and ideas you have are not that relevant, believable, or all that important. It is amazing when you put them on paper how much glamor they lose or gain once they are in front of you, and it forces you to confront them.

The next thing is to take all these ideas finding a dry erase one-month calendar is a good option that allows you edit at will. Paperworks™ is the one I use. You can fill in the blanks and see if any of it even makes sense. You look at your primary important items, which may be a job, or you realize that you may need to change jobs. You then consider the steps that make tasks more enjoyable and enhance the outcome. Next, you start adding on projects. For example, I want to put new seats in my boat, or maybe I want a new kitchen stove. Then, lay out a plan over the next one or two months to accomplish your goal. What parts of the project need to be accomplished in what order to make it work?

This is something you may want to evaluate every Sunday night or Monday morning. Doing it in a rush is not beneficial. It needs to be in a calm setting that allows you to settle your mind totally as to what's really important. The main point is that you only live today once. Once it is gone, it cannot be redone. Today you can choose left or right. What direction will you take?

If you find yourself overwhelmed with projects, you probably need to eliminate some. Realize that working full-time at something doesn't necessarily make it productive. Maybe spend a weekend every month as we did in July, camping and fishing every weekend. We fished, we floated we sat by a campfire! That helped rearrange the priorities in our lives. Find something you enjoy that is relaxing, then organize your time to plan and reset your direction in life.

I read a story years ago and it is one that I have heard numerous times about two men in a competition to see who could split the most firewood in a day. They both started out in the morning with their chainsaws revved up, and raring to go, and started cutting wood. The one woodcutter never took a break all day, with sweat running down his neck and cutting as fast as he could go. At the end of the day, the first woodcutter looked at the second one who cut more wood than he had. The first woodcutter was very frustrated with the second woodcutter saying, "You took breaks all day and sat on your tail, yet you still cut more wood than I did. How did you do that?" The second woodcutter responded very calmly saying, "Each time I sat down I sharpened my saw." We need to take time to sharpen our saw. Without doing that, we are just cutting wood with a dull saw, frustrating ourselves, and making minimal progress.

One of the items that should be a priority on everybody's list is personal health. I have one chapter dedicated to this topic. Everyone should devote a portion of their day to being healthy. It may be a 15-minute walk, it may be getting rid of your sugary drinks during the day or eliminating some of the refined foods you eat. Understand that you are ultimately responsible for your own health. If you do not make that a priority, it gets ignored and suddenly, you are sitting in a hospital bed with four bypasses and feet being amputated because you have diabetes. This is something to start on as soon as possible. It is also important to share that with our family members and children. You will never make a more important investment than in your health!

But realize you cannot make someone change. They have to decide to change what they do in their lives. You might think you oversee everybody else's life, but you can only oversee your own life.

Dr. Dennis L. Harper
Idaho, 2021

Chapter 1

"I don't know my name."

—Grace VanderWaal

Miracle, a noun meaning "amazing or wonderful occurrence," comes from the Latin *miraculum*, "object of wonder." Dig way back and the word derives from *smeiros*, meaning "to smile," which is exactly what you do when a miracle happens. To quote the American-Cuban-French diarist Anais Nin, "The dream was always running ahead of me. To catch up, to live for a moment in unison with it, that was the miracle." Just ask any rock star.

We all have definitions in life of what a miracle means. It is different for everybody. With that said I get to make up my own miracles. About 20 years ago I had a consultant ask me to write down all the things that happened to make me the person I am today. I started out "I was born November 9, 1956 in Crescent City California," a small town of 2,500 people. That was the beginning of my miracle.

We tend to find the things that define us and our purpose in life. We should view every day as a miracle. I go to bed every night saying, "This was the best day of my life," and in the morning I look in the mirror and say, "This is going to be the best day of my life." Looking back at the miracles of the last 64 years and finding defining moments makes me the special person I am and that makes me a miracle!

My memories of kindergarten and first grade helped define the direction of my life. Without realizing it at the time, those events allowed me to discover miracles. It directed me on a pathway to change the world.

Kindergarten and The Little Girl

I started kindergarten at 4½ years old. My family thought

it was okay for me to go to school early. My parents felt that having an education was extremely important, so they put me in a Catholic school starting in the first grade. The Catholic school was strict. I wore a gray tie, red shirt, with salt-and-pepper corduroy pants.

The first and second grades were together in the same room; third/fourth, fifth/six, seventh/eighth were grouped accordingly. There were about 18 students per classroom. One clear memory I have was standing in front of the school doing the Pledge of Allegiance, other things that stood out to me were: When I went into the first grade, I ended up sitting on the second-grade side for the first two weeks and nobody caught it. I was five years old. When it was finally discovered, I was told I was wrong, and Sister Bosco hollered at me and made me get back on my side of the room. I had no idea where I was supposed to be. Sister B… coming to my desk, opening it up, and saying it was a mess, taking everything out and throwing it on the floor. I peed my pants. It was one of the most traumatic things to me. I was very embarrassed.

After being relocated in the room I sat across from a beautiful little girl. Time has erased her name. She sat in the row next to me by a tall, narrow window. This girl had beautiful blonde hair that would sparkle in the sunlight. She was gone a lot from school and I never understood why. My memory of her was about March of 1962. I remember this was Easter time and I had gotten her a little teddy bear. She was dead a month later of leukemia. Being five years old, I didn't really know what that meant. There was no grief counseling or any of that back then.

In the third and fourth grade, I would sit, draw pictures, and gaze out the window. I would draw people walking in circles of radio waves to heal them of things. I am not sure where the ideas came from. There was no internet or news that talked about healing with radio waves in the 60s. Looking back you have to wonder what is guiding you. Where do those ideas come from? How do they get there? What drives you to make them happen?

Thoughts of the "little blond girl" sat in the depths of my brain until about four years ago. I had not thought about it or the reasons I had been driven in all those years. Was it the little blonde girl that drove me to learn how to heal people?

My goal when I started my practice was to get in, start three practices, get rich, and get out. I was 20 when I started chiropractic college; I had just turned 21 and graduated at 23 with my Doctor of Chiropractic degree. I had a real drive to start a practice. However, I went broke with the first practice I was in. I took a bunch of consulting courses, did different things, started back again, started making money, and started investing it. Everything I invested in, I lost money. It did not matter if it was real estate, stocks and bonds, trading futures—whatever I did, it seemed like nothing worked.

My practice was doing well, I was traveling, and putting together my own training program. I was pushing all the time, running between the practice and trainings. Later I learned that my staff were concerned that I was headed for a nervous breakdown. At that time, I had also reached a point in my marriage where having tried everything I could to make it work, I realized I was not happy. We were living together yet we weren't connected in any other way. I realized I was drinking too much in an attempt to numb myself, and I had to get out. A woman I knew helped open the door to learning what my feelings really were. In that imagery, the picture of the little girl came up. In my brain I cried for two weeks. It was like, "Oh my gosh, that's why everything I've done to this point in time has not been successful, because I had a different purpose in life."

Recognizing my purpose allowed me to make better choices. When I started making those choices with the idea of changing the world, all those doors began to open up. My teaching improved, my presentations became better. The people I meet in my life became a greater source of joy. Understanding what drove me, and what my true purpose was, allowed me to live every day as the best day of my life knowing that the next day will be better yet. It's amazing; every incident seems to build on the next and more ideas come into my brain all the time. Depending on who you talk to, we know/assume/believe that all the ideas in the world are in the Universe if your mind is open to hear them. Whether you believe in "God" or in a god, or the energy of the Universe, if you allow yourself to be open you can hear and feel almost everything that happens.

The story of the little girl; was it an emotional driver? Or was it an experience? It could have been either, or both. It was something that influenced my life so profoundly it subconsciously drove me in a direction. Yet when remembered years later it served as a wake-up call allowing me to course correct based on the memory of that experience. It's the chicken or the egg. Which came first is the eternal question, yet both are a reality. In the case of the little girl, was her purpose to prompt me to do something or was her brief life and my part in it what opened me to the idea of healing people? Did it drive me, or did I choose a course based on that event? We will never answer that question; yet it allows us to look at things in our lives from a different perspective.

Rather than labeling events as good or bad, we should rather question what impact each will make in our lives. We hold the power to determine how events will shape us, to be who we're supposed to be in life. When I think of my experiences in Catholic school, I realize I never looked at any of it as positive or negative; they were just things that happened. I believe that's probably what saved me. If I had seen peeing my pants in class as a total negative and a failure, that might have caused me to be scared my whole life. If the girl dying had been so traumatic to me that I feared emotional attachment, it would have been a negative. Instead, I developed an ability to choose my response to every situation.

I have always had a passion for talking to people, getting out, and doing things. That school experience was obviously interesting with respect to the fact that it was a very controlled and strict environment. I gained a great education, and it pushed me in areas I wasn't comfortable with. As a first grader (today), you never would have been treated that way. Did that environment push me to become the best I could be or was it simply my time to be pushed to be who I could be? It's about choices and questioning those choices. I will explore that more in my book. Anything that happens to you can be an experience—good or bad, it doesn't matter. It's just an experience. What we do with that experience is what defines us.

In this journey we have choices to turn left or right.

Thanksgiving Day 1985 found me on my knees in a 100-year-old log shed digging through two feet of snow to find something to start a fire that might keep me alive through the night. I was living my dream of hunting elk in Idaho, and **it was going to kill me!** My ego had driven me all day to walk through three feet of snow in 14-degree weather. I should've been home with my family having Thanksgiving dinner. My friend the deputy sheriff said, "You can't get lost here," slapped me on the back, sending me off in the wrong direction. This "easy" two-hour walk found me on my knees, half-frozen, in the snow, as close to giving up as I'd ever been.

Unable to fire my rifle because it was frozen, I drove my gun into the snow and got up. Thoughts of my son David, born just six months earlier, were all that kept me going. I looked around and decided, *I'm going to go left*. Turning left I couldn't see anything except driving snow, it was a total whiteout at 3:30 in the afternoon. Yet turning to the right, everything was clear, and I could see fine. It felt like God put His hand in front of my eyes and said, "You're not going that way." Going left would have led back to my vehicle, but something appeared to be telling me that I wasn't going to make it if I went that way.

Now on my knees tending several small fires I had managed to start in the rotted logs of this old cabin, I was worried that I would go to sleep and not wake up, so I set my Casio watch to ring every 20 minutes to keep me from going to sleep. I was scared that I would never wake up, fearing hypothermia would set in. I think it was more so carbon monoxide poisoning because I remember being warm at the time. I could see lights in the distance but couldn't hear anything despite being 100 yards from the road.

Forty people were out searching for me and the sheriff had warned the party, "If we don't find him soon, he will be dead." Gary, a friend of mine, joined the search around 8:00 p.m. "Look, there's a flicker of light!" The person riding with him insisted, "That's nothing, just snowmobile lights." Gary stopped to check it out anyway, "Dennis!" he yelled. I fired my last shot, shouting, "I'M HERE." I nearly died 100 yards from the road.

We have choices how we connect to people!

Twenty years ago, I watched a friend of mine dying of prostate cancer. I did not have the guts to go by and see him when I should have as he went through the process. I'm not sure why other than it simply scared me, and I felt helpless. It was a poor choice on my part. Having to live with that decision made me change the way I make those decisions today. Dealing with decisions honestly can be one of the biggest miracles.

It hits closest to you when you have one of your best friends faced with mortality. I had coffee with Doug every morning for the last 15 years. He was an alcoholic for 30 years or more. He had not had a drink in nearly 20 years. He did love his coffee, cookies, and cigarettes. I would go by his house in the morning and spend 10 or 15 minutes having a cup of coffee. He told me two years ago that the throat cancer he been treated for three years earlier had come back. The recommended treatment would include cutting out half of his tongue and part of his throat. They gave him six months to live even with that treatment. Doug refused, saying that he did not want to lay in bed having people fuss over him, and he refused to tell almost everyone else. We discussed a treatment program, and we put him on a regimen of alternative care. We took him off his cookies and his cigarettes, and he started improving.

In August, Doug's daughter came over from Europe and spent a week with him. He had not even wanted to tell her about the cancer. He confided in me that he would not live to 71. He was 70. Being able to have a great visit with his daughter, Doug started back with his cigarettes and cookies. He had lived a full life and was happy with what he was doing. In October 2018, I was teaching in Santa Fe. Before we left, over coffee he told me that his legs were starting to swell. I told him it was his kidney or heart, and we would take a look at it on Monday when I returned.

I had a dream on Friday night that Doug was lying on his back with his right knee bent up. I was comforting him as he died. We returned on Monday from Santa Fe. He normally opened the gate to our house when we returned from a trip. The gate was closed, and Doug was not at home. The family has a cabin about an hour away up the river. On Friday morning my wife and I took a trip to his cabin. They have an old cabin on a beautiful place on the Clearwater River. We walked inside and found an ashtray with one cigarette burned out to the filter and a small load of wood in a wheelbarrow. Doug was peacefully laying on his back with his right leg bent knee up—the same position I saw him in, in my dream. I walked up and put my hand on his knee and was thankful I had been with him when he died.

Learning to connect the dots of what makes magical things happen.

The miracle of the stories is the evolution of how and why I am at this place in life. It has helped me become connected with who I am becoming, and I am thankful for the energy of the Universe connecting us in an incredibly special way. The goal is to be honest with people and ourselves. The door then is wide open for all possibilities. Truly being connected to your purpose allows you to see miracles every day.

Chapter 2

"Make it simple but significant."

—Don Draper

The Early Years

My father allowed us to do what we wanted. When I was growing up in Crescent City, California, I wanted to make some money to save up for things. I wanted to buy a gun when I was 11, so I worked for two years just to save $50. I picked up bottles and cans and turned them in to the store for the deposit. I would get up at daylight on Wednesdays and ride my little Stingray bicycle a good mile and a quarter to school. I would buy two newspapers sold in town. One would cost a nickel and I would sell it for a dime; the other one sold for a dime and I resold it for 20 cents. I bought the newspapers and sold them by the bakery close to school. I would make a couple of dollars in the morning for the two hours I worked, and that was a big deal.

I remember a gentleman came up to me once and said, "Well, I'll buy you a donut. Do you want one?" I said, "Oh, no thanks. I have to stay here and work." There was no organization to my business; I bought the papers and sold them. I would also mow lawns. At that age, I only weighed 65 pounds and pushed a big lawnmower all over the place to mow yards for $3 or $4.

Apparently, I picked up something about entrepreneurial ideas when I was young. We would also peel bark from trees for chittam, which was used as a laxative. We dried the bark and sold it for $2 to $4. We were always doing something to make money. In fact, those jobs were our hobbies.

It was a quiet lifestyle in a small, isolated town. We didn't have a lot of exposure to outside ideas or thoughts, but we got to do what we wanted and rode our bikes everywhere. But the Crescent City that I grew up in doesn't exist anymore. Today, there are two pelican bay prisons and a maximum-security prison. The town has 15,000 residents and it even has a McDonald's. The crime rate has increased.

I was there during the tidal wave in 1964 that was the result of the historic 9.2 Alaska earthquake. The night that it happened, I woke up at 12:01 a.m. and went outside to see the town in flames. We had to evacuate town while my father helped with the search and rescue team. We didn't see him for two days and questioned whether or not he made it. Three waves inundated the town and wiped out the first five blocks closest to the shore. Twenty-seven boats sank in the marina. My grandfather actually rode the waves out in his boat. Eleven people died, most of them from a single boat.

We bought one of the sunken boats, a 44-footer called the Idle Hour. It was wooden; we put plastic in it and raised it on skids. We worked on that boat every day for three months that summer, digging sand out of it. It got to be so much that I never cared if I went to the beach ever again. Adding to our previous entrepreneurial pursuits, we worked on it enough to make a profit. But between the environment and the times now, those opportunities just don't exist anymore.

Red and Dad

Red retired from his business in 1957. He was a hunting fanatic, which is also one of the reasons why I live where I do. If Red hadn't taken my father to Idaho, I wouldn't be living here today. I remember Red would go on guided hunting trips during the year and dad would always say, "Why is he spending his money to do this and that?" Well, Red had the money and he wanted to do it, I thought it was great. But dad always kind of poo-pooed Red's trips.

It comes back to my view of money, which was you worked hard, worked a lot, saved money, put it away, and then you could retire and do what you wished. There was a bit of a guilt issue I had with doing fun things and not feeling like I was goofing off. If I took a trip and went to Sedona, Hawaii, or Mexico, I would feel guilty about not working more. That all came from the interplay between Red and my father.

I don't think a lot of people look at why they do what they do. It's rather fun to actually tease out what causes us to make the choices we do. My frustration was the fact that I felt I was supposed to work a lot, yet I wanted to live a balanced life. Back then, people didn't talk about living a balanced life and were just told to work hard. Working smarter (not harder) wasn't even a concept at the time.

I watched the people around us who had their own businesses actually retire early and do what they wanted to do. Today, I am in a profession that allows me to do what I want *and* get paid, so I have the best of both worlds. It took me a long time to realize that. I'm doing something I really enjoy. Every day is not a labor to go to the office or teach. Instead, it's a joy. I get to meet people, live where I want to, work with people, and work as hard as I want to work, to make the money I want to make. I'm not punching a timeclock either.

This makes me think of my dad. He had been working for Caterpillar as a product support manager for over 30 years. Several months before Christmas, another company bought the local dealership out in Eureka and wanted to move his job to the dealership in San Francisco. Dad didn't want to move down there, so the company fired him the week before Christmas.

What was interesting about it is my Uncle Ted (my dad's identical twin), who actually worked at a different Caterpillar store, had quit two years before and went out on his own, buying and selling equipment. Ted made way more money than my father and dad kept saying, "I need to do what Ted is doing." This forced my father to do it, which was a good thing, but it was obviously a stressful proposition. After a year of doing that, I remember telling Red that my father felt so guilty about not punching that timeclock anymore. He made four times the amount of money the first six months and still felt guilty not having to punch in and out each day.

It took my father over a year to get past it. I remember calling Red again and asked if he could talk to dad and let him know that he was doing well. But my father couldn't let himself believe it because of the rules he was raised with. He felt the need to be conservative about when to spend money and what to spend it on. My dad grew up in Princeton, British Columbia without a lot of money. Dad and Uncle Ted would go hunting but they wouldn't shoot a duck unless they could kill two ducks with one shot. They only had so many shells. In the same vein dad said, "Dennis, don't be as conservative as I've been. You need to go do things." I struggled my whole life with what he did and said, trying to break out of those boxes we get ourselves into.

After several years, my dad made quite a lot of money and then retired. To me it was a sad thing because he ended up developing Parkinson's about 15 years before he died. He retired in Yuma and would go golfing, have Happy Hour in the afternoon, and that was the extent of his day. It was sad watching him because he used to be a vibrant individual who was always on the go. All of that stopped after retirement.

With watching this lesson play out, it got me to thinking what retirement is and why we retire. What is life anyhow? Again, it should be a balance. We tend to get caught up in the rules we get from people on what we're supposed to do and not do, what we think is right and wrong. Our parents, friends, and society give us all of these messages about which direction to take. I look at the way I've lived my life and the things I've done that were probably more on the correct side but still had the anchors that I had carried until I allowed myself to finally let go.

I'm still learning this, and it's important for us to keep learning. Keep digging to the root of why we do what we do and what we should do with it. That's the challenge right there. You can call it an awakening or an evolution, but we have a choice. We have the choice of simply growing old or growing brighter every day.

I had a patient the other day who I have treated for 35 years. She is nearing 80 and asked me, "How do you grow old gracefully? I hurt, I can't do the things I want to do, I'm not in the shape I want to be in. My husband and I can't be intimate anymore because it hurts too much. He's having problems keeping himself together." I sat down with her and responded, "It's one of those things that we have to evaluate daily a little better than we do now."

I heard the statement years ago, "If you coast, you coast

downhill." I call it the Naked Mirror Test for my patients. You get up every morning, look at yourself naked in the mirror, and see if you're happy with yourself. Obviously, you're the person who can change it. If you need help, you can start exercising. You can do alternative care treatments. You can do bioidentical hormones. You could do thyroid treatments. You can do a lot of things to help you to become healthier. But unfortunately, when you reach 65 and draw Social Security, you're also on Medicare, which pays for nothing to get or keep you healthy. Now you're stuck in this paradigm of not having money to invest in your health, and just enough money to buy health insurance that covers acute care, not <u>health care</u>.

Truly, we don't buy health insurance anymore, we buy injury insurance. Unless you invest in yourself somewhere financially, you're going to go the way the system expects you to go, which is an aging system. You have choices. Growing old gracefully is a mindset and it takes some work. You can make it fun in the process and reap the results.

The Why of the Why

I visited my mom in Yuma a while back. It wasn't the best experience; in fact, it felt like a vacuum that sucks the life out of you. If you look at your environment, having people that drag you down or build you up, how does that manifest in your life? Looking at this aspect is really tough for some people. Sometimes it's the spouse that drags you down. Your job might not be the best fit. Where you live isn't the best place for you. Running to a different town doesn't solve it, either. You have to have the mentality to understand why you're moving to a different town. When I train doctors, one thing I emphasize is to learn the why of the why. If you have a patient that has diabetes, well, why? "Well, because my blood sugar is off." Well, why is your blood sugar off? "My diet is wrong." Why is your diet wrong? "Well, because I'm lazy," or, "I'm depressed," or, "My parents told me I should do this, so I'm doing this." But why do you let that affect you? When I look at the symptomatology of patients and discuss it with them, why is the why happening? It's a bigger question than just looking at the surface.

I think life is really important in that way and it's my cause for frustration. The frustration I had is that I didn't understand *why*. I didn't know *why* I was working so hard. I was working to retire because I had been given the rules by somebody else—and that wasn't it at all. I was supposed to get up and enjoy the day. I was supposed to live a balanced life, but we never heard about that concept back then.

Now, my wife and I plan a year in advance for fun activities that we enjoy and make us happy. That's probably the other part of it right there. My mom and my previous spouses—I've had several—all came back to the fact that people look at us and say, "Oh, you guys are so happy and doing so many fun things!" I respond, "No, we did fun things, but I wasn't happy." The big difference between doing fun things and being happy is enormous. You can go to Las Vegas, you can go to Asia, you can go to Europe, to Ireland, and go to fun places, but you might not **be** happy.

I spoke with a lady yesterday and she said, "Something is wrong with me. As I get older, I really don't want to go places. I don't like to travel that much and I'm happy." Well, then she's happy at home. But me, I've got the travel bug. I like to see and experience new things all the time. It's a curse and a blessing. It would not be constructive for me to sit around all the time. I have to grow constantly, and I think that's probably something I've learned, and it makes sense to do.

Going back to what my folks told me back in the 1980s when I was trying to build my practice and make it work, my parents would come up for a month to hunt after dad had retired. I had to go to 10 classes a year in San Francisco; it was a three-year program I was enrolled in. At that point in time, I was on the State Board of Examiners, was seeing 90 patients a day, traveled once a month to do that seminar, and worked six days a week in my office. I was halfway through the program at this point when I was sitting around the campfire with my parents. I told my mom, "Oh my God, I'm so excited! We're learning this and we're changing and improving these things." She looked at me and said, "Well, it's been a year and a half. Haven't you learned everything yet?" Some people will say, "Oh, people get older.

They get more set in their ways." Is that something you want to do? Do you want to be set in your ways, or do you want to live life every day to its fullest?

It doesn't mean you have to work every day. It doesn't mean that you have to play every day, either. But it means that you have to *experience* every day. Again, this is where my frustration lies. It's not so much the goal you set to achieve; it's enjoying every step of achieving the goal. It's about enjoying the journey, but it doesn't really sink in until you look at what you're doing every day. My mom would tell me, "We'll just see where tomorrow goes," but I don't find that acceptable. However, that view is prevalent among many people still.

I'm the type of person that if I want to do something, I'll try it. For example, one of the things I wanted to do 25 years ago was trade futures and stocks. This was before the internet was set up to the capacity it is today. To achieve this, we had to buy a satellite dish and down feed of a link that would give us a 5 to 10-minute delay of the market. That was as close as we could get at the time. I went to a class in Las Vegas from a top futures trader and learned what they taught. I put $10,000 in an account and saw what I could do with it. The program that I learned was way too complicated, so I decided to trade T-bills, which cost about $1,400 for each contract.

We tried trading in the beginning and that didn't really make much money, but then I developed my own system. I would get up in the morning at 5:00 and flip on the TV to look at gold, bonds, and the S&P 500. At that point, I would make a decision to buy or sell. I would buy at 5:30 a.m. CST, call the broker up on the boxy cellular phones at the time, put on coffee, and I would buy and/or sell what I wanted. My goal was to make $250 by 7:30 that morning and then go to work.

I would go sit in the hot tub with my coffee and have the phone with me to see if my investments shifted. At that point in time, I was trading once or twice each morning. The broker called me up at the end of the month and told me I was trading too much. I asked if he could give me lower fees on the trades, which he was fine with doing. Eventually, I traded three or four times every morning. There was a month where I actually had a 100% return. I had beaten everybody else and others were actually following my trades.

Yeah, I thought I was doing something right here. But the main broker called me up and suggested that I should stop trading so much and to slow it down a bit. You see, some mornings I would make a couple thousand dollars. He told me to trade less, so I tried a month of that. But I lost everything in that next month—because I listened to what he said.

How influenced are we by other people instead of following our heart? I had a hard time imagining that I was a top trader in the whole company. We don't give ourselves enough credit sometimes. It goes along with the whole box of rules we've learned from others. "You're not smart enough. You're not tall enough. You're not good-looking enough," but a lot of times it doesn't matter. We have what we have, and we have what we need, yet we still listen to others.

Because of this, I've become selective about who I listen to and what I take to heart. I got out of trading because I realized it was too much of a rush. To get fired up like that before work and then spend 10 hours seeing patients, I realized there were too many negative things going on. But the point is that I definitely did what I wanted to do. I experienced it and knew I could do it, so it was a win. I walked away with a win while learning something, which is the most important takeaway. People get involved in something and possibly face a loss along the way. The question is, did you learn something from it? For me, the money was immaterial. It comes down to how you did with the venture you chose to pursue.

I have patients whom I have treated for 39 years now, so I've watched the decisions they have made and where they have ended up because of those decisions. It's like a mirror; I look at myself and where I'm at now. I was 23 when I started practicing, and I still feel 23 years old. It is interesting to look at people who come in who are 80 and I'm thinking, "Oh my God, how did you get to be 80? I'm 23." What is more interesting is seeing the kids who come in that are 20. I get to look at them and see what they are going to be like in 40 years unless they change what they're doing. How do you get across to them what is going to happen? How invincible did you feel when you were 20 years old, not realizing that the "coast" could kill you—or make you? It depends on what you do with it.

Bob and Ernie

When I took my entrance exams for chiropractic college about six or seven months before I applied, I had to go down to Berkley. I remember taking the exam, stepping outside, and meeting a gentleman named Bob. He was almost exactly 10 years older than I was. He said, "I'm going to chiropractic college," and I said, "Wow, me too!" The first day of school, I walked into Western State and there was Bob. During our early days in school I learned several things about Bob; Bob had two children, a wife, and was extremely intelligent. He was a geologist, so I hung out with him a lot. Scholastically, he was able to get through things easier than I could. He could take a chemistry test with ease and would get an A. I had to study all week to get a C. Bob knew how to take tests and play the system; he was sharp at doing that. But I was just a hard worker. I lapsed scholastically because I didn't feel that I was the brightest one on the block. I had a 3.4 GPA in high school and managed a 3.0 GPA in college. However, I showed Bob how to live life.

Ernie, who was about five years older than me, and had an IQ of 168 was a math whiz. He graduated from the University of Oregon with straight-As in math. He was actually a genius. I had scored a 95% on the math section of my ACT, so I'm no dummy, but I wasn't even in the same boat with Ernie. We were in different leagues.

Bob and Ernie helped me get through chiropractic college, but I taught them how to hunt, fish, have fun, and relax. We complimented each other, creating balance during school. But the lesson was interesting to watch as we all went off into our practices. Ernie stayed in Oregon, Bob went to California, while I went to Idaho. Of course, we kept in touch, reconnecting, and hunting together for many years.

After about 10 or 12 years of practice, Bob walked into his office one day and called it quits. He served his wife divorce papers, closed his practice, and disappeared for a year. Ernie joined a practice with someone who worked the system. He and his partner were prosecuted under the RICO Act in federal court. Ernie plead states' evidence and quit practicing for 25 years.

It was interesting watching two people who were smarter than me but couldn't stay in practice. It comes back to balance. I worked during the week, I had time I took off during the year. I took weekends off to go hunt, fish, or do whatever. Bob and Ernie would just work, and they never really owned that balance I tried to give them. Looking back on Bob and Ernie, they were both great people. It was interesting watching that evolution of what they ended up doing in life. Ernie was highly intelligent but needed to be managed. Bob was unhappy, looking for an answer somewhere, not realizing he was the problem and the solution.

Are you a problem or a solution, and how do you figure that out?

Chapter 3

"What comes easy won't last, and what lasts does not come easy."

—Unknown

I've had patients ask me certain questions, which always prompt me to expand my thinking, which is a good thing.

When the topic of death comes up, there is always the question of timing. Which leads to the question: Can you speed up death? That comes from several things. I have watched people die at an early age. For instance, we will talk in more detail later in the book about the young boy with leukemia dying. Why did he die? A young girl who had a skateboarding accident at 19. She fell on her knees, scraped them, and went to the emergency room. The doctor scraped gravel out of her knee, sprayed some antiseptic on them, and out of the blue she dropped dead.

But then there are people in horrendous accidents with every bone in their body broken, yet they survive and recover. Again, someone scrapes a knee, gets an infection, and dies. People try to commit suicide and don't die. Over the years, I have seen different examples of people who try to shoot themselves and miss, they cut their wrists or overdose on pills and do not die.

All of us at some point wonder when we might die, when our time will be up. You have to wonder when and how your time will come. My mom would always tell me that I seemed to have nine lives, and I've used six of them so far. I've had horrendous things happen and I must question why I'm still here. I just talked to a lady in the office this morning who loves to ride horses, I have been officially banned from doing that, having taken several falls off the horse. Once I was bucked so hard it ripped the reigns out of the bit and I went head-first 25 feet over a hill. All that happened was I had dirt on the side of my pants—not a scrape, scratch, or anything broken. I never even lost my hat! The last time I was bucked off, I went eight feet in the air over the horses' head and landed flat on my back. I landed in the only place on the entire six-mile trail that was flat. No boulders, nothing. I wasn't even sore afterwards. Now, how does that happen? Are these incidents meant to be messages or course corrections if you will, or a commentary on our life about things we should or shouldn't be doing, that happen in our life? Messages on what we should or should not do? Or is it telling us that we have a different purpose in life that we should be doing and working on?

I fell in my shop 12 feet off a ladder and landed on my head on the concrete floor. I don't remember eight hours, had 23 stitches, broke a bone in my face, and cracked five ribs. When I went to the ER, I looked at my x-rays but didn't remember any of that. At 2:00 in the morning, all I remember is a big male nurse in my face saying, "You can go home now."

So why didn't I die when I had that fall? Generally, if you took 10 people and dropped them on their head from 12 feet, it is going to kill nine of them. I read an article the other day about a lady that fell 33,000 feet out of an airplane and lived. Let's look at why that happens. Obviously, I will not be able to answer that question, but we should be asking ourselves about it. It's okay to have a question and not have the answer for it, sometimes it's more important to understand the question.

Can I postpone death? Can I speed it up? The question is how is *when* you die really determined? Is it preordained or is it something that is knitted into the fabric of life as you travel along? There have been many philosophical arguments about that and what's going to really affect what you do.

I call my mom every day and ask, "What are you up to?" Invariably she answers, "watching golf or baseball," with the unspoken message being "I'm just letting whatever happens in life happen." I always think of George Burns who played God in the movie GOD. He was asked, "How long are you going to live to?" George said, "Well, I've got things scheduled till I'm 101, so I'll live through at least what I'm scheduled to do."

In this book, *Solving Life*, you have to look at the beginning game and the endgame, and then put into perspective how to live with the path you've chosen, or choose a different path. I think it is important to look at what seems like many random ideas and put them into the context of choices. Maybe those choices are preordained by what we have been introduced to, but what if they're not. Maybe—It really is just as simple as turning left, or right today? Then the question becomes, "What are the differences between turning left or right?"

I go to bed at night, looking back at the day and say, "Today was the best day of my life," savoring the experiences I had, not choosing to classify them as good or bad. If my office burned down today, would it be the worst or the best thing that happened? It might be the best thing, because it may make me do something I was not going to do before. You must learn to have a good attitude about events that happen. That is the conclusion I've come to. There is no point in getting upset about it. Can you alter what happened? You cannot alter other peoples' actions. You cannot alter a meteor strike if it happens either.

There was an orthopedic friend of mine—one of the best orthopedists I knew. He was a neat guy and had eight kids. He was riding a snowmobile and out of nowhere a tree fell and killed him. How in the hell does that even happen? We were at the reservoir fishing last week and heard this horrendous crash and saw a tree come down. If we had been under that tree, it would have crushed both of us, but we were not there. Things happen.

With that said, if you evaluate your day every evening and say, "Okay, today was the best day of my life, and these are the positives I can take from it," even if you take two minutes to list it in your head or write it down. What happened today? Surprisingly enough, someone actually backed into my building while recording the content for this chapter. What happened? Well, I met a neat person. So that is a positive. Maybe it will make me do some work on the building, maybe I need to paint it or put better signage out. Finding the positives amongst what superficially at least appears as negatives gives you the opportunity to wake up the next morning, look in the mirror and say, "This is going to be the best day of my life. I am free to choose right or left in any given situations."

Have you ever been in a situation where you wanted something either to happen, or not to happen and you tried to "force" the outcome in one direction or another? Say I decide to put a gun to my head, and I am not supposed to, will the gun go off? Obviously, we are not going to test that theory out. We are going to make choices that make some logical sense in the process of what the Universe or God puts in our path.

A tool I use is to evaluate tomorrow, the night before. This sets a framework into your brain that allows you to successfully launch into the next day. We take all these instances, experiences, and ideas and we say, "What choices do I have today?" I can choose to have the best day of my life today. I can choose to look at what that feels like. Am I pushing a dead horse or am I on a path that makes sense? Many times, what we feel is the correct path may in reality be a detour that we've taken without being entirely aware that we've strayed from the path.

To sum up this chapter, I believe the real take-away is learning to recognize the signs when we stray from our path, (exploring on the journey is fine, and can even be enjoyable and rewarding) but pushing uphill in the wrong direction is frustrating, stressful, unhealthy, and unproductive. By allowing ourselves the grace to change course without judgement or self-incrimination we are free to navigate at will, choosing left or right without fear or judgement. In turn, allowing each of us to go to bed every night saying, "Today was the best day of my life, and tomorrow will be even better!"

In conclusion, I believe the choices we make begin with the realization that we have choices. We cannot change other people. There are events that are outside our ability to control. We can, however, control our response to them. We have the power to control our choices and our responses and how we perceive each. We can choose the people we hang out with, the books we read, and the TV we watch, making sure each has a positive impact on us. At the end of the game we should be at peace with the choices we've made.

It's time to work on your endgame.

Chapter 4

"Believe that tomorrow will be better than today!"

—Unknown

Tonight, as we reflect on the day's decisions, we need to look at how those decisions will influence tomorrow. Who decides what tomorrow looks like for us? We are in a time of extreme stress right now. Fear, doubt, uncertainty, anger, and radical departure from our 'normal' have everyone on edge. Rather than looking forward to tomorrow, many of us go to bed fearing what tomorrow will bring. It is more critical now than ever before for us to recognize that we are responsible for tomorrow. Not the government, not your spouse, not your kids, not your neighbor, your boss, or anyone other than you "me, myself, and I." That is who tomorrow rests on! The challenge is deciding what you want to make tomorrow look like or let someone tell you what your tomorrow will look like. Do you want to be happy? Do you want to be sad? Do you want to be rich? Do you want to be poor? Those are our choices.

And the best part IS: I choose my tomorrow!

How many times have we looked ahead at tomorrow with a sense of apprehension about something that is on our schedule? Often times we worry all night about a thing only to have it end up really being either not what we expected at all or just not a big deal. For instance, a patient called, they were concerned about a rib they had had adjusted. The doctor that treated the patient worked in my office at the time, having not done the adjustment myself my immediate thought was, "Oh, they're going to sue the office!" I woke up in the morning, looked at the patient's file, and the records indicated that it had nothing to do with what I thought at all. Considering I have never been sued, was this really a reasonable conclusion to jump to? Probably not, but I took the bait.

My plan was that I would go into the office in the morning, do A, B, and C, and alleviate the situation. Everything was fine, the paperwork was fine, the doctor's work was fine, and I discovered that the patient was simply driving too far for care and wanted to drive less—a simple solution. It was not an issue at all. Needless to say, I did not get sued; the point is I allowed myself to worry needlessly when I could have chosen differently! That is where reflection on today and reconnaissance for tomorrow can be our best friend or our worst enemy! We often make up things that we worry about part of the night, when in reality we are using this as a distraction to avoid the real issue.

When I do my mile walk each morning, I use that time to ask myself, "Okay, what do I want to do today? Do I want to keep seeing patients? Do I want to cease being a doctor?" After 40 years, I realize that I'm actually enjoying what I do more than ever! So, I choose to come into the office. Instead of saying, "I hate my job. Why am I going into the office?" I choose to make every day the best day ever! I was thinking this morning I may stop seeing patients in a year. I could make a choice today to say, "It's time to go on to my next adventure."

That ability to choose comes from an evaluation of the day before and APPRECIATION of the things that happened, allowing me to wake up tomorrow, and decide what I choose the day to be like. When I look at the steps on "retiring from seeing patients" or stepping into the next level of my life, I think of a close friend of mine. Two years ago, he was under threat of losing his license, practice, wife, and the money he had saved over 40 years of practicing. He finally surrendered his license at the age of 65, and it was time for him. I talked him through it, and he was able to maintain his retirement and his marriage. He is now happy and living life. The stress that he had created by desperately trying to hold on to his license is gone. He had created the stress from the actions taking place around him.

I told him, "Find the good things you can do and make the best of what you're doing now." He was financially secure; that was not an issue. It was purely the stress of losing his license, instead of framing it as trading in his license for something better in life. The choices we make today allow us to reap the rewards tomorrow!

I believe looking at the complete picture is the answer. It is what gives you the fullness of life for which you can be thankful. Becoming distracted by the micro takes the enjoyment from the macro. Tomorrow can be what I choose it to be, and I challenge each of you to embrace making those choices. Remember, things that happened yesterday are only things that happened. The clarity of tomorrow may change what we think today was. Go to bed, being thankful for things that happened in your day, and realize they are going to give you a better tomorrow—if you choose.

Chapter 5

"Ideas come from everything."

—*Alfred Hitchcock*

This concept hit me hard. Where do you get ideas from, and how many are really ideas? I do not think we examine that very closely. An example of this would be when I went to the flower shop to purchase something for my wife on Valentine's Day. Walking into the shop with no clear idea of what to get, a particular plant jumped out to me like it was the only plant in the shop. Scanning around, I had made it a quarter of the way through the shop and just froze, all my attention focused on that one plant. There was no real connection that I felt; I just knew that was the ideal plant to get. The odds of our small flower shop having this plant available and the odds of me walking in and finding it; well if it had been a lottery ticket, I'd have been a winner for sure! Shirley loves this plant and had in fact wanted one for years yet never was anywhere that she was able to have one. It is a plant more suited to warmer climates, seldom seen in our part of the country. How does that even happen? She cried when she found it on the counter Valentines morning!

Why do you choose to go left or right? Why do you decide to look up, look down, stop, say hello to someone, or not greet them at all? Think back to a time you didn't say something to someone and regretted it a moment later. I think our life comes down to the point of too many times we stop and say something we shouldn't and don't say things we should, and we know it in our heart immediately. How much does that actually change the direction of our lives? It doesn't matter if it is positive or negative; it just changes things.

This is the same as when we went down to Utah to meet a gentleman at a lab, he never showed up. It was an amazing array of decisions, ideas, and circumstances that are sparked by another's actions and words, how we process them, and what action results from that. It could be something that changes the direction of our lives. You can overcalculate or undercalculate, the goal is to recognize the feeling inside to know that you're doing the right thing. The results may not be immediate, either. It could be six months, a year, or five years down the line that a decision finally comes full circle.

What is trusting your gut? It is trusting what you must do. An old chiropractic saying is, "Top, down, inside out," referring to the energy that goes into the body. It comes from the top down, goes back up, and then out. When you walk into a venue that has open seating, how do you choose where to sit? You consider convenience, maybe safety. Sometimes you want to be seen by others and sometimes you prefer privacy. Maybe you sit somewhere because you will have better service or to avoid a cold draft. Maybe it's the view outside, by the bar, or near the kitchen. Ideas come from logical conclusions to something you want to solve. On the other hand, ideas come from asking if there is a place you should really sit. Where is the fulfillment in the choice you make?

Think about the decisions you make and backtrack it. This is something we don't practice very often. I was walking down the street yesterday and had to see the economic advisor for my community. What side of the street do you choose to walk on? Do you mix it up a bit? Why did I choose that? From what I could tell, there were no consequences to the decision. Other times, you make directional choices and end up running into a person or something that subsequently sparks a thought process. I run into occasions and issues with people where I'll be inspired to research a subject. Maybe someone asks me a question.

Why does water run downhill? We just observe that it does, but do we understand why? Why does water do this when the planet is constantly spinning? Thoughts and ideas are influenced by the people we meet, the books we read, and the TV we watch. All our decisions are based on information we have or have been given, but more importantly, what other influences come into play? This is where a question comes into play. Does it come from a divine source, the Universe or does it come from the summation of our experiences that initiate a thought process to solve a problem or to discover a way to move forward?

In my practice, I have created treatments that nobody else has and developed new modalities. This ability comes from the culmination of my experience and ideas, but more important is the ability to put those pieces together and decide a course of action. Going back to the plant on Valentine's Day, I did not have a basis for that decision in my experience of life. My knowledge base of plants is simply knowing that they are usually green and have flowers. But the knowledge to make the decision to buy that plant had to come from somewhere. For Shirley to feel as strongly as she did about it tells me that we're connected, but how so? Is it just by sharing experiences or do we share thoughts with others without being aware of it? I think we take for granted some of the things we do, not realizing what inspires us to do them.

My wife and I travel a lot. I will be on an airplane, hear it rattling, and then theorize that we may be headed for a crash. Five or six years ago, I was helping a friend who has an outfitting business. I'll go out and cut trails with him or put out bear bait in the wilderness. He also has horses. We were going to go horseback riding on Labor Day weekend. Two weeks before that, a patient of mine was thrown off a horse, had been dragged for a bit, and died. The week after, my good friend Jim was riding his horse in the wilderness. It bucked up and he came down on the saddle horn, splitting his pelvis apart. He rode bleeding internally, almost losing his life in the process. The sheriff had to go in to retrieve him and transported him to the hospital, saving his life.

I'm going into this horseback riding trip remembering what people say about bad things happening in threes. I was anxious about this horseback ride and was riding a horse I hadn't been on before. This was a tall horse, and I am only 5'6", so my legs don't reach far enough around the horse to offer me a grip. This horse fit me well, seemed to be well-tempered, and I was comfortable. We went out, cut more trails, camped two days, and were on our way back home. It had rained the night before. As we rode along the narrow trail, the horse was excited to get back home practically prancing around. Soon enough, the horse starts to go off the trail and it's nearly a 200-foot drop straight off the trail. My horse was sliding down the hill! Fortunately, I had the wherewithal to dismount immediately. He was about four or five feet down and continued to slide. My impulse to simply step off as the ground rose up to meet my foot on the trail side saved us both that day! It allowed him to regain his footing and get back up on the trail. If I hadn't gotten off the horse and just hung on or flexed funny, I would have died.

Once we got back on the trail, I was totally calm, and the rest of the trip was a piece of cake. Had I fretted about the experience to make that happen or was I aware that something was going to happen, and acted on an impulse? As far as I was concerned, this was the third horse incident that I have survived. But where do we get those feelings from? Do we have a feeling that things are going to happen as a natural course of events or do we make things happen, thinking they will play out?

A story we can consider is that a woman marries an alcoholic, abusive husband. She gets out of the relationship and says, "I'm never going to marry an alcoholic again." Of course, she marries another alcoholic and it's the same situation. She gets out of that marriage and into another one. The woman repeats, "I'm not going to let this happen." I read years ago that if you tell your subconscious that "it's **not** going to happen," it will happen. Why? The subconscious mind fails to recognize the negative words.

How does the brain separate that or how many things happen for a reason? This is the ultimate question I don't think we will ever be able to fully answer, even though we will continue to wonder. The question is how to use these thoughts to our advantage and not bury ourselves with them. We tend to make up a lot of those thoughts and feelings, but we have to put them somewhere. How do we analyze those thoughts and go forward?

How do we sort out the thoughts of, "I'm going to fast today," or "I need to call this long, lost friend today," and why do we sort those out? It comes down to the fact that we need to sit down and parse out what drives us. Are we greedier than we should be? Are we sad when we should be happy? Are we overconfident when we should be more realistic? We tend to run along, pushed by the ideas that we have been given by others. It rolls over our ability to actually make clear decisions. It's not about the best information we have; it's also the information we get from the Universe. Something is present to make that happen.

Some people say it comes down to your belief system. There are some who say that our lives are pre-determined, and events will happen no matter what we choose. There's the option that we have choices to make in life. But we do not have the ability to backtrack our lives and make a different decision. Is an event predestined to happen even though we have free choice? That is the ultimate question.

How many times have you made a gut decision but regretted it later? Have you harassed or yelled at somebody or done something that you knew was wrong, either because of the rules you live by or rules received from others? Maybe you affected someone's life in a way that you are unaware of. Maybe it was an honest error. The fact is that we don't have the opportunity for do-overs and have to live with our mistakes. Yet sometimes we are faced with a harrowing decision and have done everything possible for a good outcome, yet it doesn't happen despite our best efforts.

How do you make the decision that you're going to shoot and rob somebody? Where does that decision come from? If you come from a relatively moral background, chances are low that you will carry out the action. Another person has no boundaries set in place yet firing the shot and robbing someone might be the outcome. Does this idea come from God or from a dysfunction of experiences? Are the decisions and actions the second person made put in play by God to affect the lives of others, thereby influencing their decisions?

My daughter dealt with some issues when she was younger. I remember coming home from the office at lunchtime and trying to talk to her. I stood on the deck and thought to myself that I should go back to work. But no, I also had the thought that I should talk to her for two minutes. I *chose* to speak with my daughter. Later, as I was driving down the hill a half mile to the road, I saw a logging truck on its side in my driveway with logs spilled all over. Now, if I would have left when I originally intended two to five minutes earlier, I would have collided head-on with that logging truck. Where does the thought process actually go for me to consciously decide *wait... stop? I should go talk to my daughter for a minute.* Now, was that put in my brain to talk to my daughter or was it to distract me from making a decision that could potentially kill me? How do you sort that out?

Do the actions we take in the morning affect decisions later in the day? Is it going to change the way we interact with others? What do we do with it? Is the solution of life increasing our awareness that this possibility exists? It's a starting point to look at what influences you. People use prayer as a means to talk to God or the Universe because they are open to listening. God or the Universe are likely talking to you all the time, depending on your belief system. The question is, are we listening?

If you're on your way to work and swing by the bakery to get a donut and a train runs through the crossing you would have taken had you not stopped, were you predestined to stop, or was that a random unrelated decision? We need to realize the potential exists and be more openminded and listen to our God or the Universe.

About 35 years ago, I was on a flight with an empty seat by me. An older gentleman boards the plane. He looked around and was pleasant to everyone. He looked at me and said, "I'm going to sit by that young man right there," and proceeded to do so. He was the man who invented the valve that took us out of the iron lung era. After that flight, we corresponded for years afterward. That one decision he made resulted in a huge impact on society. His decision to sit next to me impacted my own life. But who benefitted more? Was it an equal benefit? I believe everything should be a win-win. If it isn't that way in business, I don't want to do it. Realize that not everyone has the same idea of what a win means!

We have opened the door. Now it is your choice: left, or right?

I have always been a highly driven, motivated person. If I do not have something to do, I'll create 10 things to do. I remember my dad telling me, "If you're bored, I'll put you to work," so I was never bored. How many times do we get stuck on potential boredom? It is the same thing with depression. We get stuck on not wanting to make a choice or having enough confidence to make one—so we make *no* choice. That just adds more fuel to the fire for depression to set in. And of course, there are chemical and food additives that contribute to this downward spiral. If you're drinking a gallon of whiskey a day, that's not going to help anything. But what drove you to make the decision you did? It is all about choices.

Do we wake up and exercise this morning? "Nah, I'm feeling kind of lazy, but I should still exercise." Rather than beat yourself up all day saying you should have exercised, forgive yourself and make up your mind to look forward to doing better tomorrow! Again, it comes down to recognizing what drives your decisions and why. It's all a question of why and what for.

If we take a moment to review things that have happened in our lives, some are the result of distinct recognizable choices we have made, others are just a series of seemingly random occurrences void of choices that have brought us to where we are now.

Chapter 6

"Don't judge my story by the chapter you walked in on."

—Unknown

If I jump forward to life today, I can honestly say I am the happiest I have ever been. In my journey, you could say that I turned over many rocks in my search for just the right cocktail. Many of the ideas and directions in my life have been the result of being extremely goal oriented. I was driven from an early age, driven to succeed, driven to work hard or suffer feelings of guilt that in turn drove me to work harder. It was a never-ending hamster wheel that I couldn't' break away from. I spent time doing fun things, hunting, fishing, and traveling, yet when I looked back on my life, I was shocked to realize that I had never been genuinely happy. The constant drive to do fun things effectively masked my unhappiness. "Fun" replaced real joy. Fun simply distracted me. I never understood what happiness was. I would say things like, "I want to marry a woman. I want to buy a new stereo. I want to buy a boat. I want to go on a trip to [wherever]." But none of that was really happiness; they were just things; they were fun but served only to fill the gaps where happiness should have been.

I figured that in setting my goals when I was younger, I would attend college, continue on to chiropractic college, and get out as quickly as I could. I started college at 17, and by starting then, I went six and a half years straight through school and got out. I never took summers off or time off. I figured that a woman would be basically a distraction, so I decided that it was great to chase girls, but I did not want to catch one until I was 25. I figured that was a good age because I would have my business going, I would have everything done, and I would be out the door and ready for a happy life!

It was challenging going through school because I would date several women. There was a point the summer before I graduated chiropractic college where I had three different women ask me to marry them. Okay, so I ended all three relationships. I remember meeting a woman in November that came into the store I was working at during the last year of college. She said she was moving to Australia in two months, so I thought she was a safe bet. She was not going to stay around, so I didn't have to worry about it. We could date and do some things.

Then she decided she was going to stay. She was seven years older than I was. She had latched onto me and I thought it was okay. I was so tired from six years of college that I don't think I had the energy to say, "No, this probably isn't the best thing to do." After she met my folks, I thought they liked her, so I reasoned being married was a good thing for a professional to be. So, we got married. Many years later I found out that they were hoping I would not marry her—I was 23 at the time, but what did I know about being a professional? What did I know about being a doctor, what did I know about being married, or about life? There are no classes that teach you those lessons.

I was going by other peoples' rules that I assumed existed, had heard of, and thought of. How many times in life do we live by rules that we have been told are the way we should live? I always like the comment, "*They* said this," and I've always asked, "Who in the hell are *they*?" I went on living my life going by what they told me. We did have two wonderful children, David, and Sarah, whom I am blessed to have in my life. My marriage lasted about seven years, but I was totally unhappy. What "they" don't really tell you is what you do when you just aren't happy. I was raised to believe that once you are married, you should stay married period—no matter what—that was part of my Catholic upbringing. In the same respect, I was not happy. It went back to the goals I'd set. I wanted a relationship that worked well, but I had forgotten about having a relationship that would make me happy. That difference led me on a trek of three marriages.

It took coming out of the last relationship after being married for 21 years, finally able to admit I was not happy. Again, other peoples' rules said, "Oh my gosh, you guys do so many fun things!" It finally dawned on me then that I was not happy. When

Shirley (my current wife) and I talked and listened to each other, I was looking for happy feelings in my past. Talking about it, I could not bring up a happy feeling in my entire 58 years. There were lots of fun things I did, but I was not happy. If you like to do fun things, I am a fun person you can do them with. I like planning fun things and set great goals. If you take a trip with me, I have things going on all day and you can plan what you want to do, or something we all want to do. I am great at doing that—but I was not happy.

How do you sort this out? Where do you even start? I think the challenge is looking first to find happiness in yourself. Unless you are happy with yourself, you are never going to be happy. You're in a relationship and you like to get up at 6:00 in the morning while your partner prefers to get up at 8:00? So, do you go to bed earlier and start getting up with them at 6:00? Do you say, "To heck with it, just don't bug me when you get up"? Do you like to eat at the kitchen table, or do you like to eat in the living room? Truly, you would like to sit at the dinner table, but your spouse wants to eat in the living room. Those are simple examples, but these differences become more pronounced when it comes to other levels of the relationship, this type of disparity in reference to sexual relationships causes much frustration, even small things like holding hands, sitting by each other, saying, "Good morning, honey. I love you." How important are those things to fulfilling your needs?

Life would be much simpler if we knew what made us happy before we looked for people and things to make us happy! To evaluate that, we have to learn how to break down all those items.

Signs and Symptoms of Happy or Fun Things

Obsessive-compulsive behaviors. This is taking extreme measures to do something versus not doing it at all. I have friends that decide they want to take on a hobby. One person in particular comes to mind; he took on long range shooting as a hobby. He bought a custom-built, expensive rifle, the most expensive scope, built an 800-yard shooting range at his house, and bought the most expensive shells. When I look closer, I see he had problems with alcohol. Do we transfer things from one obsessive-compulsive or addictive behavior to another to replace the destructive behavior with fun things? Obviously, alcohol was a problem and to his credit he was able to stop that harmful behavior and redirect it to other things. He became a fanatic fisherman as well; bought the best boat, all the best gear, and spent all his time on the water. By doing "things" we avoid having to face ourselves, and that is the problem.

When you look in the mirror what do you really see? I have joked about the naked mirror test that I tell my patients to try. Many people take this to mean looking at yourself superficially to see how you "look" when in reality we should use the mirror to examine the inside of ourselves first. What's on the inside has a direct correlation to what others see on the outside. If you find it difficult to look in the mirror it likely has more to do with the inside than the outside. You could become a competitive weightlifter and spend all your time at the gym. But making your body look good can even destroy relationships. Bottom line, you are still avoiding examining what makes you genuinely happy.

What does happiness really mean? Happiness means that you are comfortable in the skin you wear, and how you wear it. It is feeling comfortable with the person you are and the person you are becoming. It is also the comfort of being able to look at others without expectations because you realize it is their choice as to how they live their life, and you're living your life the way you want to. A lot of people who are not happy want to tell everybody else how to live their lives in order to feel better about themselves.

What is the cure for this? It again goes back to the naked mirror test; you must start with yourself. But you must do things for the right reasons. This is where spousal relationships come into play. I have seen men who want women to have breast implants, want them to diet, or cut their hair a certain way. In turn, these women become somebody else for their man. I have also seen it play out that men take on extra jobs to buy their wife extra things or move to another area for her. There is a point where a person is happy doing that with no regrets, and that's fine; however, that is the exception rather than the rule. There is usually a little dig in there, and those digs can grow and grow until finally the relationship falls apart. Trying to untangle all the pieces we become over the years, being one thing for this person, living by this rule from someone else it's no wonder we find it hard to look in that mirror! Where do you even begin? You need to find some space where you can figure out who you really are. I do not mean run off to Alaska or disappear for a year to accomplish this. What I mean is just to have a place where you take 15-20 minutes every day and think about why you do what you do.

Why do I get up at a certain time? Why am I going to work every day? Why am I not going to the gym or making it a priority? Why do I make poor choices about what I eat? Am I drinking a fifth of whisky a day? Sort out and honestly look at what really makes you the person you are. How many rules did you get from your parents? I have struggled terribly with those. You are supposed to work hard until you die. You are supposed to keep your nose to the grindstone—words I have always heard from them. How many times do siblings drive you in a direction because they want something out of you? Carrying all those things soon becomes a burden, a burden we continue to carry so we don't disappoint or to prove a point. At the end of the day the person we've let down the most is ourselves!

I heard a comment years ago—something I discourage staff from doing is to ask a patient, "How are you doing?" Sixty-five percent of people do not care how you are doing and 35% hope you have a problem worse than theirs. So, which category are you in? You need to ask yourself that question. Ideally, you've made yourself a priority and are healthy and genuinely happy. This then frees you up to honestly care how others are without the need to make excuses. If we are making excuses for why we can't, won't, don't do things, we're not happy. I do not have the complete answer other than we truly must learn to look to ourselves. We each come from a different place and to be able to look deep into our own souls is as individualized as we are.

So now is the time to get NAKED. Look in the mirror! There are hundreds of different formulas out there to arrange goals and priorities. My list below is an example of what I do for myself to

help organize my thoughts, priorities, and choose left or right.
   THE FORMULA:

(This is an example from a recent list I created to organize my thoughts and actions in a direction that would allow balance in my life and all the associated items around me.)

Number one: Chiropractic office. Breaking down the parts of the office and identifying priorities.

Number two: looking at the financial parts IVs, Dr M, blood work, injections, biologic allograft.

Number three: looking at viability of doing the virtual conference. The amount of time involved and the profitability.

Number four: Classes for patients: The viability of expanding to twice a month advanced learning.

Number five: Budgeting system for the office.

Virtual Conference:

- Numbers of hours available to work on it per week
- Financial viability and cost to put on
- PowerPoints to be done - time involved
- Details of initiating and funding the project
- Conflict with personal trainings for doctors. Incorporating personal trainings with virtual conference.

Working with political projects:

- Priorities of projects. Dworshak Project.
- Farming project
- Funding programs for the forest. Education.
- Political advancement of going forward with elections and being elected to a position.
- Evaluate time with political projects. Set up so much time

a week and call it good.

Personal projects: Including the cabin and projects around the house. Doing more improvements on the boat.

Time expended to finish the book.

New projects next year. Put each project under a strict evaluation process before taking them on.

Look at time with the legislature this fall. Look at helping improve some of the chiropractic legislation.

Talk with all the board members on the IACP. Go forward with legislative things if it works into my time schedule.

Work out personal time so there's so much time allotted every month.

Take time with all the kids. Schedule time for a monthly event. Evaluation of DBS viability.

Talk with Jolene and business plan.

Look at filming time in Utah. Maybe a good opportunity to talk with everyone.

Personal business with Legally Mine and all the easements to the properties.

- Easement to our house
- Bruce's easement

Prioritize work and improvements at the house considering money over the next several months.

- Number one: basic rooms finishing. Including my office at home.
- Number two: includes the carport build-out.

- Number three: a tossup between the living room and pergola covered enclosure.
- Number four: the fan in the living room. Need to clean my shop out as much as possible.

This is a working model about when I sat down and put all the things down that weighed on me. It is a good thing to take all the pieces of the puzzle and put them on a piece of paper. Then sort out the things that do not belong on the piece of paper and figure out how to accomplish what needs to be done with the projects that are left. The important part is to keep from adding more stuff on that competes with getting stuff done that is more important.

Chapter 7

"Adventure is worthwhile!"

—Aesop

This event was the epitome of my life. It was the culmination of a dream, a dream that had driven my choices most of my life, as far back as six, eight, or 10 years old. What was "the" thing you dreamt about? Was it to being a rock star, a football star? What was your dream, your passion, and how much did it drive your life choices? My passion was hunting and fishing. They inspired me. I would dream about the feeling of what I would get if something happened in the positive: kill a big buck, catch a big fish. The feeling of it, the excitement, and the anticipation of it fueled my passions.

All those years, I looked toward the fulfillment of that dream. Think about something you like, something that motivates and excites you, gives you that warm, fuzzy feeling, maybe it makes your heart pound. Are those feelings still waiting to be realized, or are they feelings that you look back on with relish, or were those dreams left behind, never to be realized? Either way, whatever the case, ask yourself why. Did the decisions you made assist you in fulfilling your dream? Or did your choices cause you to leave the dream behind? It's funny; when I thought about 'The hunt" a lot, I wouldn't sleep all night.

"The hunt" that was my dream, the perfect hunt. I thought about it a lot, was it, an elk hunt, or a deer hunt. I would lay in bed at night and dream of what it would feel like to shoot a big bull, a big moose, a big elk. I would visualize the weather, crisp and cold with a bit of snow on the ground, and the freedom to focus solely on the hunt. No distractions from business, my wife, the kids, other things in my life. Just the luxury to live completely in that single moment, and it always made me enthused to get up and go to work the next day. I wanted to work towards that goal.

It takes a special tag to hunt a moose in Idaho, it is considered a once in a lifetime opportunity. It could take four, five, or up to 10 years to draw a tag, or maybe never get one. I found an area I wanted to hunt and fortunately I knew the outfitter who hunted that area. I checked the books and found out that the biggest moose in the state had come out of that unit so that is where I applied. Four tags a year are drawn for that unit. It was a back-country unit and if people did not have horses, they wouldn't apply. Maybe only 10 people would put in for the drawing. It took me two or three years before I drew a tag. Once I drew the tag, I wondered when the best time would be to go. The outfitter said that in November all the big bulls were together, and they were done with their rut. There was snow on the ground for easier tracking. Either way several things were required to make it perfect.

My dream began in earnest on November 3rd the location was 90 miles from my home. The camp was six miles back in the wilderness and we slept in tents. We would ride 10 to 12 miles a day up in the high country in the snow. It was about 20 degrees and we had three inches of snow in the morning—the perfect weather for my dream hunt. I hate riding horses because I wind up hurting so bad. We ended up cutting a set of tracks the first day that were just huge, 30% bigger than any other moose track we had seen up there. We did not see the big bull, but there were fresh tracks in front of us. There were two bulls together. We cut the tracks again the next day. We had seen a bull each day, up to 40-inch bulls. They were nice, but nothing I wanted to shoot. The average antler spread in Idaho is about 25 inches for a bull moose. I had all week, so I wanted to take my time and not rush. I had 10 days off, so I wanted to stay until I shot the moose of my dreams. The third day, we go up the trail and there are those big moose tracks. You could tell the moose immediately because the tracks were so much bigger. We began tracking them through mid-morning.

The next morning, on the trail in front of us was the smaller bull, he was 42 inches. My friend shot it, so I knew exactly how big those antlers were. Rich our guide said, "Dennis, go back on the trail and look. The bigger one is standing to the left there." Usually, I have trouble getting off a horse because I have short legs. I slide off the saddle until I touch the ground, not graceful at all. I was so excited that I literally leapt off the horse with my gun in hand. I ran back onto the trail and there he was, standing there, he was huge!

Shaking with excitement, adrenaline rushing through my body I get ready to shoot. As I'm loading my shell into the chamber I "short stroke" the action. In a hurry, I failed to get the shell into the chamber. Rich, sitting quietly on his horse is watching me. I line up my shot at 60 yards, it wasn't a great shot, but I knew anatomy well enough to know that the shot I had could take him down. I pulled the trigger so hard I almost jerked the gun out of my hands! CLICK! Nothing! I took a breath, calming myself. This time I observe the shell going into the chamber, realizing my earlier mistake. Fortunately, I didn't panic. I lined up the shot, took a breath, and squeezed the trigger. The moose did not even move. I hit him just under the spine, missing the main artery. He just stood there. I jacked another shell in as he turned. I shot again hitting him in the shoulder and down he went. He never took a step—it was a perfect shot.

I turned to Rich, "He's down! I got a good shot, it's good!" We tied the horses and walked toward the moose. I walked to the spot where he went down and there was no moose. My stomach dropped. The dog ran past us on the way to the site, I was off by 20 yards. We found the bull and it was massive.

My plan was to do a European mount, where you take the antlers off the skull and just mount them. We looked at his beautiful black, silver-tipped hair, probably an eight or nine-year-old moose—in his prime, at the peak of his maturity. If he had been any older, the points of his antlers would have come down and begun to round off. We looked at each other and said in unison "mount that whole head," which is something I did not plan on doing.

We sat there and I opened a bottle of whisky I had brought just for that moment. We had a toast to celebrate a dream come true! Every facet of the dream had been just as I'd visualized at least a thousand times. It was about 25 degrees out, a little bit of snow, no wind—a beautiful day. We had all afternoon to just cape and bone it out. We made four piles of meat and caped the antlers out. I was going to pick the whole head up and it probably weighed 200 pounds antlers and all. We cut the antlers off and finished up about 3:30 in the afternoon. It was the third day of the hunt, we tracked it for three days, we rode it out on the third day. It was everything I dreamt of. It was perfect!

The horse freaked out, so we could not put the antlers on the horse and ride out. I put the antlers on my back to pack them down the first half mile to the main trail. Realizing how heavy they were, I was thankful for the ozone injections in my left knee which made the pack easier. I decided to walk the mile back to camp. I was literally in a dream trance. I sat down a couple of times and just looked at the antlers, stroked them, and realized I could not have dreamt of a better outcome.

We returned to camp before dark, had a nice barbecue that night with refreshments. It was amazing, and the excitement was beyond surreal. I woke up the next morning, realizing it was no longer a dream. The fourth day, we rode out. The outfitter was such an expert at his job that everything went perfectly. I timed it from when we tied the horses to when we headed down the hill with the meat all loaded up, it was 19 minutes, and we are talking about a whole moose. I rode back to town that day, drove home, and arrived later that night.

I had Wednesday, Thursday, and Friday off. As hunters must report to Fish & Game, I went there on Wednesday. The officers all came out of the station, opened the tailgate, and their mouths dropped. It was one of the largest moose shot in 15 years in the state, so it was a monster. I returned to my practice with antlers in hand. Another doctor was working that day, and I was content telling the story over and over to patients for two days. I reveled in the opportunity to relive the excitement again and again!

The outfitter told me, "I know where we can get this processed and caped really quickly. I want to use it for one of my shows in February." I told him that would be great, so we took it to Missoula, Montana. In January I received a phone call from the taxidermist. He told me, "Oh my God, this thing is huge!" I replied, "Well, it's a moose." He said, "No, you don't get it. I could not fit it on a Shiras mold."

There are three classifications of mounts for moose. There are Shiras, Canadian, and Alaskan. A Shiras mold stands 36 inches from the wall, and an Alaskan mold stands 56 inches from the wall. He had to put it on an Alaskan mold to fit my huge bull. He said, "I have an Alaskan moose I'm also doing, and your moose is as big as that Alaskan bull." The bases where the antlers come out of the head were within one-eighth of an inch of the Alaska world record. It was *that big* a moose.

 I hosted a Hunt of a Lifetime party at my house in March. The weather had been rainy and cold. We had invited 75 people over to the house, suddenly, out of nowhere the weather turned 75 to 80 degrees that day. We had an outdoor barbeque of moose meat, refreshments, a bonfire, and had the unveiling of the moose for everybody at 3:00 in the afternoon. I recounted the story of my dream hunt to our guests.

 Have you ever thought about the purpose behind those "dreams"? Is there actually a purpose or are they meant simply as a means of distraction? I assumed that everyone experienced them just as I did. It wasn't until I met my wife Shirley that I realized that not everyone thinks the way I do. For example, I love to cook. I will look at a package of hamburger and think about the taste and sensation I want to experience when I eat that hamburger. As I described this to Shirley one night over dinner, I noticed a strange expression on her face. Puzzled, I stopped and asked what she was thinking. She shook her head and told me she had never heard of anything like that in her life. It was my turn to be puzzled. "I thought everyone thought like that," I said. I learned not everyone does!

 When I cook, I begin with the sensation I'm trying to create, then I think about the best way to achieve that sensation. I've discovered that fasting really accentuates the appreciation for the feeling I want from the food, taste, smell, texture, and even the mood or emotion I want to achieve. It's the difference between eating and creating a culinary experience. This same mind set can easily translate to other aspects of your life as well. Creating a richer fuller, more rewarding experience out of ordinary everyday events. For example, your dream might be that you want to buy a new car. Why do you want a new car? What is the feeling you are looking for when you buy it? I think by framing life differently, by putting more focus on the feelings and sensations the experience evokes makes it feel larger, fuller if you will. The reason is often the thing itself doesn't bring the expected satisfaction nearly as well as taking the time to savor the emotions you want from the experience. I think we miss a lot in our lives by looking for *things* to make us feel a certain way, rather than looking for something that fits the feeling we want to have.

This is why I am continually fascinated with "the why." I am constantly admonishing doctors to "look at the why of the why" when treating patients. It took me years to process my moose hunt and what really made it perfect. The time spent looking beyond the superficial afforded me opportunity to relive the joy I experienced that day. What is your dream, and what feeling are you looking for from that dream? By focusing only on the dream, we lose sight of the feeling we are looking for. Without the feeling, the dream may be disappointing or unfulfilling in the end.

I know the greatest regret people in nursing homes have reported is they wished they would have done more things in their life. Ninety-five percent felt they put off their dreams, hopes, and wishes until too late in life, and they missed out on accomplishing them. Whatever the reason, be it physical, financial, or death of a spouse preventing them from achieving their dreams, the sad reality is it never happened. The lesson is if you do not do it now, it may not happen. Today only happens today, it doesn't come back tomorrow. You have to be realistic. You cannot just throw everything away and go do it now. It's about the balance, about planning to make things happen. The time to start is NOW!

November 7, 2011 was the day I achieved my lifelong dream. My dad died on November 7, 2016. The irony of the whole thing, as I looked back on it a few years later realizing only in retrospect that both happened on the same day, was the fact that my dad had been the inspiration for that dream. How often in life do you have a dream that surpasses any dream you ever have? How often does that happen? This had surpassed my dream!

Chapter 8

"Life is what happens when you're busy making other plans."

—John Lennon

This chapter is dedicated to and is a transcript of a presentation I gave in January of 2020 to 200 doctors in Phoenix, Arizona. The occasion was Dr. John Brimhall's annual Homecoming conference. Having attended some of his trainings early in my career, he has been a mentor to me, and an icon in the field of Chiropractic. I speak on many topics to a wide variety of practitioners; it is something I enjoy. I have spoken at venues with doctors including some of the top orthopedists and researchers on stem cell procedures to small patient classes at my office. Speaking in front of groups is not for everyone, but it is one of my passions. To view one of my talks, go to my **harperozone.com** website. Enjoy!

"I want to tell a story this morning. I cannot do that until my wife takes my phone. I find that I am never lost because someone always tell me where to go. I lost my watch years ago and decided I did not need another watch because I have four women in my life that tell me where to go all the time. What an amazing place. I get dressed in the morning, by my wife. I get told what time to be at work, what time to go home, and who I am seeing every day by my fantastic staff.

Do you ever wonder why you do what you do? Four years ago, I had a startling revelation because of my wife. When I was in first grade, I went to Catholic school, I remember sitting by this lovely little girl with blonde hair. I remember in March 1962 looking at her blonde, curly hair; the sun was shining through the windows and her hair was sparkling. She had the most beautiful smile. And I remember I bought her a little teddy bear for Easter. She was dead a month later from leukemia.

We had no grief counseling—we had nothing like that. That memory was the revelation! It lay buried in my subconscious for almost 60 years. Early in life I would draw pictures of healing people by having them walk through radio waves, this was fourth grade. Where does that come from in the 60s? Somewhere someone was guiding me all along. My goal was to retire at 25. Everything I did in those years, financially was with early retirement in mind. I should do this or that and retire. It all went south. Why? So, I could be here today to talk to you.

The experience and the lessons were making me who I've become allowing me to have the best life ever! You let God or the Universe guide you to where you need to be, and you will be where you need and should be.

'I am just a chiropractor. What the heck can I do?' You have the best education out there to treat these people. You've got to learn to take the tools you've been given and make them work. That poor lady was in an accident; she was unconscious for a year. Oxygen deprivation to the brain. They had pulled the plug on her to let her die and instead she woke up. She came to me for chiropractic adjusting. What on earth was I even going to adjust on her? I mean, she was in spasm with all her muscles. There was no motion.

I am going to open this window for you to see what you can do. Rebuilding the body and true regenerative medicine. We hear that term all the time, 'regenerative medicine.' Okay, what is regenerative medicine? Detoxing the body, diet considerations. I am going to call it preconditioning the body. Hormones—we have got to deal with hormones. Charging the body. Mental balance. We have heard all these things this weekend already. These are all going to get put together for you. Age with beauty and grace. Here is a big one: make a plan that a patient will follow.

How many patients come in and do not have the will to do a quarter of what you tell them to do? They say a patient remembers 5% of what you tell them by the end of the week. A doctor when I teach in classes I think remembers 3% of what you tell them.

The choice today is yours. Do I go right, or do I go left? Now start with detoxing the body. Processed foods we know must go. I am going to tell you a lot of stuff you know already, but I will put it into simple terms for you. The best solution is to take anything with a label on it out of your diet. Glycosides, glutens, steroids, and NSAIDs. We have an opioid crisis now, right? Because it is self-induced and facilitated by the pharmaceutical companies. Does this get in the way of a patient improving? Dramatically. Dairy limited or none. Sugars and carbs—again, I am telling you stuff you have been hearing all weekend. Check your water sources. This is probably something you have not thought about a lot. Mold and radon in houses are an issue, the environment you live in is extremely important to evaluate and look at. Air in the house—we run an ionizer that also ozonates our home and office as well.

Dental work in the mouth—you want the mercury out of your mouth. Everybody knows that or should know it and remove it. Chelation is an option to detox—oral, IV—it depends what you need. We have options. We use a sublingual solution. There is a lot of detoxes on the market. OSH has a detox kit. We are working with them to give you what we call the "Preconditioning Packet."

Dietary considerations—fresh is best. Eliminate processed, sugars, and carbs. I am doing something I am going to talk to you about that you may not have seen. I call it "seasonal eating." I practice in an area where we have the Nez Perce Indian tribe. Their diet forever was 95% fish and roots. You introduce sugar into their system and alcohol, what happens? They cannot process it. The Eskimos eat mainly fat, and my understanding is an Eskimo's genetics allow them to produce Vitamin C. If I took an Eskimo and a Central American native with a diet of fruits and vegetables and I switch them, do you think either would survive well on those diets? They might both die.

Now, we look around this room, how many genetics do each of you have? I am Dutch, Irish, English, and half Italian—I've been told, but who knows what is in the woodpile? So, what do I process? Fats? Sugars? What? I think we need to look at how our body metabolizes to find an eating program. A one-size-fits-all diet does not work for everybody. You need to be aware of that and see that. I have seen people get sick on the Keto diet. I have seen sick vegetarians. I have seen all these people sick for different reasons. So as a doctor you need to be conscientious on what is really causing the problem.

Healthy fats—I am all into fats one meal a day. Air and water being clean. Cancer risk factors can reduce by six times by keeping your blood sugar below 90 – a simple thing you can look at to do. Vitamin D levels above 70 lowers the risk of cancer by five times. Two simple things you can look at. Prolonged fasting, we have talked about. It promotes self-renewal, regeneration, and immune protection. I have patients do intermittent fasting if nothing else. Eat between noon and 6:00, two small meals, and we try to control what they eat. They will do that. I have them do a 24-hour fast once a week and once a month a three-day fast. There are different variations of one day to three days to five days and Dr. Mark as we know does 14 days in a row, twice a year. Fasting has different levels of things that are physiologically affected, so please look at that.

Key nutritional points—how to put nutrition into the system. We're going to talk about ozone. Why? Because it is something you can all do, and your patients can do at home. Patients will ask, "What can I do at home if I've got money to do stuff?" What are things I would recommend? "Get an ozone machine." You can bubble water, you can drink it, you can do ear insufflation, and help the brain. You can do a rectal insufflation, vaginal insufflation. It is something you can do at home every day. You can ozonate your house and clean bacteria and mold out of your house. IV ozone is the next level with a trained doctor. Fasting, prolonged/intermittent. Magnesium is important. Vitamin D, and K2 are simple ways to start.

Now how many of you have worked with OHS? We have a Preconditioning Packet you can order online now. I do not give people a lot of supplements. I will tell you three to four items would be the max I give people. How many people stay on supplements that you put them on? I recommend magnesium, Vitamin D, K2—they stay on that. It is amazing how many people I have put on magnesium. If you will take nothing else, take magnesium. I think we all agree with that.

Hormones—how many of you do or have had your hormones tested here? Do proper hormone bloodwork. Look at ideal ranges, not reference ranges. I took my Vitamin D levels over a year ago;

it was at 25 in March 2019. My wife and I use a peptide called Melanotin it is a weekly injection. I usually sunburn very easily. In July we spend every weekend on the boat. I spent all day out in the sun for 12 days in July and never sunburned once. My Vitamin D levels went up without taking Vitamin D to unmeasurably above 100. The peptide kept me from sunburn and helped utilize the Vitamin D. The FDA has taken it off the market.

A lot of people struggle with their Vitamin D levels. I am wondering if the peptides are going to make the body work better. There is some literature on peptides. The Russians have done lots of research in past years on peptides. It is not a drug so not much research is done in the United States.

Hashimoto's, we know is out of control. We have talked about the thyroid drops, the iodine testing—we do extensive thyroid testing. I have an MD in my office, and he does all my hormone and allergy work. Pellets are an option with hormones. Troches and creams are an option. Fasting will increase your testosterone, so realize that is an option when working with patients. Allograft (stem cells) can help. You will not hear me say stem cells because it is not accurate terminology. We use a biological allograft.

Charging the cells of the body. We know that a pulsed magnetic frequency was originally developed by NASA to keep the astronauts from losing calcium from bones when they went into space. There are several personal units on the market. Eliminating EMF waves is important. We know it screws us up. We wear cancellers as Dr. John shows you to do. I wear an EM canceller all the time when I travel. We have them set up at our house and our office both to cancel the EM waves in our areas. Earthing—great fun. You will hear me talk at my conferences about earthing. When doctors come to Orofino for a training, I get them in the dirt for an hour so they can calm themselves, finding balance.

Most docs are all wound up like tops. You need to find a place in your life, in your world, where you can re-modulate to a balanced frequency. Have you read much of Tesla's work? Tesla said he could build unlimited power sources from the Earth itself in a tower and transmit power out, and we would all get free power! There is still one existing tower left and they are building another one in Texas. The Earth has a tremendous amount of power. But the problem with it is the magnetic charge has decreased by 80 times since the times of the dinosaurs, so we supplement the charging of the Earth. We need charged cells for positive health, so we use PEMF.

This is our dirt time. This is my classroom that I teach at up at our cabin in Idaho. I live in Northern Idaho, a little town of 3,000 people. It's always interesting; people say, "Why are you there? You should be somewhere else, and you can make more money." My busiest day a year ago, I saw 90 people in a day. I have people fly in from all over to get treated, but I live there because it's where I get my ideas, and the dirt time is what does that for me.

This leads us into mental balance. You have heard me talk about it, look at it, so how do we change it? It's easy to say, "I'm depressed. I am happy. I am this, I am that. I'm whatever I am." Today is the absolute best day of my life. Right now, is the best moment in my life and tomorrow will be even better yet, because I make the choice. What are your choices? Right or left?

In five years, you become the summation of the people you meet, the books you read, and the TV you watch, and the talks you do. We talked about YouTube talks, talking to patients. I have learned so much from talking to patients over the years. How many times do you tell a patient they should do something, and you do not do it? Are you talking to your patient or yourself in the mirror? It is like, "I should be doing that." Look in that mirror every day.

Dirt time—find a place to reconnect to the earth. You will love it. I will go up and I will split wood. I have a D8 Cat I work (play) on. I have big toys. Read positive books. Hang around positive people. I've let people go in my life that continually drag me down. Time to evaluate the people around you; what they feel like, what they make you feel like. How many people in your life make you think you must do something you don't want to do? How many people build you up to feel you could do anything in your life? You need to find those people and maybe cut some people loose. It is a hard one to do. I have cut how many wives loose? Four? Yep. So, I have the most wonderful lady in my life now, Shirley. You will see her this afternoon. She helps me do what I do best!

Spending seven minutes a day being thankful rebuilds brain cells. There was actually study done on that. Is that crazy? I am thankful every night when I go to bed that I had the most amazing day ever, and I wake up in the morning and I may feel a little groggy or a little sore. Sometimes I will get up, look in the mirror, take a big breath, and say, "Today is going to be the best day ever," and I go forward—every day. How many of you can do just that simple thing? All of you can.

Give freely without expectations and it will come back tenfold. You have heard that before. It is written in some literature I have heard about. But how many of you truly can give without any expectation of return? Truly? How many times? Oh, I will give you this cup. Maybe she will give me her phone. Learn to give 100 percent with no expectation in return. My wife says I give too much, and she is constantly at my back. "You know, you shouldn't be giving all of this stuff away." I am not wealthy financially at all, but I am happier than heck and people think I'm extremely wealthy. I always laugh at it. But does it matter to me? Not for the joy I give people and the joy I get back from them.

Homework: A nice book to read [*The Power of Vulnerability*, by Brene' Brown, PhD]. I listen to audiobook tapes when I travel, so I will listen to them and go over them. It takes me a couple of times to get through the books because I fall asleep half the time. *Barking up the Wrong Tree* [by Eric Barker] makes you look at if you are just running your life in circles. A lot of times you feel you are walking against a brick wall every day. It reaches a point in time where you have got to change that. So that is your homework. Read those two books.

Dirt time. I take some good friends of mine, Brenden, and Audrey camping every year on Labor Day. Brenden is one of the top IV instructors for the naturopathic groups. He is a good friend of mine. I married the two of them a couple years ago. Brenden looks forward to dirt time, he has a busy practice, teaches all over the world and serves as a consultant for doctors all over the country. I'm always amazed at watching what 4 days in the dirt does for him.

My credentials are kind of interesting; I am a State Senator in Idaho—I served in the Senate, filling in for my friend, Skip Brandt. You get to keep that title for life. I am also a minister, so I could marry you or bury you—your choice. I served 12 years on our state chiropractic board, I have written a lot of laws and rules, in our state, and one of my expertise is medical malpractice. I am the doctor's protector; I litigate for the doctors and do witness testimony for NCMC (a major malpractice insurer). It's something I've been doing for 30 years. My expertise is standard of care, so I go in and talk about this. Keep that in mind, what standard of care do you need to do treatments? Much depends on your licensing. I work with dentists, naturopaths, and MDs on malpractice defense. And, just so you know, I carry no malpractice insurance. Kind of ironic that I do that. I do not own anything anymore; I gave everything away—seriously.

Age with grace and beauty. I have women coming in that want bigger breasts, their knees are going bad, but they don't seem to care. They will spend $5,000 to $10,000 on their face or breasts and not even worry about their knees going bad. I see it all the time and it is comical. There is a balance of being as beautiful as you can be and as healthy as you can be, ideally, they balance out. You need to teach people.

Sexual health. Enjoy your life to the fullest. Vaginal rejuvenation—you probably do not think about that much. I could tell you about some of these techniques. You can make a 60-year-old vagina as healthy as a 20-year-old vagina. Is that important? If you are 60 years old, it might be. Prostate health—most every male will die from prostate cancer if something else doesn't kill them. We work with some of the best sexual health people in the country. I work with, Dr. Beth, she had a urologic oncologist in her clinic and is one of the top sexual health people around. I work with a lot of MDs; I teach many medical doctors, it helps to know things I can share with them, they may not know. It has made me understand better a lot of ideas I've had.

Bladder incontinence. Is that an issue? Sneeze, pass gas, pee yourself? They are not supposed to go together, but they do when you do not want them to. Do you want to look at fixing those things? Increased sensation and control—that is always a good thing, I use ozone injections, PRP, and biologic allograft with great success.

Joint health is important. Most people have degenerative joints, knee conditions, old surgeries, back pain, neck pains, carpal tunnel pain, hip pain, heel spur pain and other conditions. What if I told you that in 30 seconds, I could reduce carpal tunnel symptoms by injecting a point on the side of your biceps muscle? There are things out there when you start looking at anatomy and physiology with a different light that get amazing results. My goal is to change your world today. The list goes on and on. Degenerative conditions, autoimmune disease, and cancer—they're all the same thing. They are the body going south on you. Let us turn it around today.

This year is my fortieth year in practice. There are less than 10 licenses older than mine in the State of Idaho. I am hitting the Top Ten. I will be number one in another 10 years. I worked with Gonstead, some in the 70s. I took 12 Gonstead seminars before I got out of school, and the most people I've adjusted is 100 in a day. —I'm kind of a slacker—I still adjust 30 to 40 people daily. I love adjusting people. But you can change things around, getting better results faster.

I get up in the morning and do a mile walk (rain or shine, snow, or sleet). It was 17 degrees at home when we left this week. I get up, do my walk, come back, and do 20 minutes on a vibration table. I use the vibration table for stretching and Shirley makes me go to the gym every night for an hour and work out. It is all good for you.

This is what true regeneration of the body is. One of your healthy, basic stem cells will build every tissue in the body as it's needed and signaled to treat for a reason. It'll regenerate brain, nerve, heart, lung, skin, hair, nails. They know now that you could actually regenerate the brain. You didn't know that. There are some new studies out that indicate you could actually regenerate all the tissues in the brain. They never thought that would happen and actually found that it can. At birth one of your stem cells will produce a billion healthy cells a month. At age 30, about 20,000 a month. Kind of going downhill, isn't it? At age 60, 200—unless you cheat. Just sitting here, we are dying at the rate of 300,000,000 cells a minute. The goal is to activate your body to regenerate its own stem cells faster. It takes five to seven years to rebuild the body. Using Biologic Allograft how long would it take to regenerate back to age 25. We are working on dosing amounts to do that.

The brown fat you have heard me talk about. Quickly—this is where it came from. I came up with the protocol from listening to a doctor treating Parkinson's with a stem cell product. Injecting at the base of the skull into a muscle near the brain, by the vertebral artery, under ultrasound guidance. And I thought, "I am not going to do that!" That is scarier than I want. He was injecting the base of the neck hoping the cells would go into the brain crossing the blood brain barrier. We know that blood supply for the muscles does not go to the brain, right? But he thought if you got close to the brain and hit the muscle, it would go to the brain. I thought to myself, "Why don't we find a better way to do that that makes more sense?" Do you know the difference between brown fat and white fat? Brown fat is the highest metabolically active source of stored stem cells in the body. It serves as a storage bank. When you run out of steam, get cold or you need to boost your metabolism you have a reserve stored in that bank of brown fat. White fat does not have nearly the concentration and is also where the body stores toxins. If I can stimulate the brown fat to regenerate new metabolically active stem cells and go out into the body to dedifferentiate and heal the system, is that going to help?

The trifecta: ozone, biologic allograft, application delivery methods. Say I get a patient with a chronic knee that comes in and I have had lots of doctors that will take—and I'm going to call it from their point, stem cells—stick them into the knee, and the knee never gets better. I have heard this complaint forever, as far back as eight or nine years ago. Patient paid $5,000 and was not any better. Why didn't he get better? Because we did not stimulate a cascade effect of healing to happen.

Now, I say ozone for a reason. The reason is we need an injury to cause a reaction, to cause a signaling system, to go to the blood with a message to signal stored stem cells, to go to the area to heal. I use ozone with our injections to irritate the tissue. Does that make sense? If I stimulate (irritate) the tissue, then deliver some products (biologic allograft) to your stem cells to activate metabolically active stem cells to then go out to regenerate your body I will get results. Inflammation activates your native stem cells. Your body has a signaling system within the red blood cells. You can pull red blood cells out and stick them back in causing a reaction, signaling other red blood cells. Amazing stuff out there if you read the literature. Transmigration is what it's called. Blood supply—you need blood supply to make it work. You want healthy tissue, not scar tissue. As we get older, we injure an area, we get scar tissue. We get no regenerative changes. There is no gas left in the gas tank to make healthy tissue.

Amino acids are the building blocks for healthy tissue. We use amino acids with all our joint injection procedures—and ozone to stimulate tissue health.

Educate your patients with realistic expectations. I appreciate Dr. Johnson saying, "I will not do a procedure on you unless you take responsibility for your health." I want to make the same point. I have told patients in the office "I'm not going to treat you until you take your health seriously" You are just asking for failure treating a patient that wants to make you responsible for their health.

Walk the talk. You know, it's pretty hard to tell a patient that you need to exercise when you smoke and weigh 300 pounds. You know it and I am just stating the obvious. We need a wake-up call. I call it the Naked Mirror Test. Every morning stand in front of that mirror naked are you thumbs up or thumbs down? Next is to start your family on the program for health. They may be resistant. It may or may not work. A person will only start a program if they decide to.

Build the most amazing team. I teach about 12 classes a year. I go to offices; we do private trainings. We have DBS for products. You should be drinking the Kool-Aid.

I try everything I tell you to do. I have shot every part of my body with Biologic Allograft. I tell people I have done it all, and you need to learn to understand everything out there if you want a health clinic that gets people better. People are sicker now than ever before.

You must draw a circle around what you want to do, what is your passion in practice. What do you want to be when you grow up? Most of you here will practice until you die because you love what you do. Add pieces on to make it even more fun yet. I have more fun now than I have ever had in my life, and I feel like I am just starting. I am almost giddy with the fun tools. You saw some of the ozone stuff we did in the last two days on people. Pretty dramatic, isn't it?

This concluded the presentation I gave. It can appear a little disjointed and part of it is just for professionals. I try to use terms professionals and lay people can understand. I hope this chapter opens a door and gives you the ability to ask more questions. This book is giving you permission to ask more questions and be in control of your destiny

Chapter 9

"It is health that is the real wealth, and not pieces of gold and silver!"

—Mahatma Gandhi

In this chapter I want to touch on healthcare, the expectation, what it really is, and what it has become in this country and to some extent the world. Most people who have an open mind or through personal experience have experienced an awakening to the realization that healthcare today doesn't have much to do with health. It is not a one size fits most, it has little to do with getting well if you are ill, and most times treatment is dictated by your insurance rather than your physician. Our healthcare system has in fact failed us miserably! This chapter will only touch on the high points. An entire book can be written on this topic alone.

When I grew up, I went to the doctor and the dentist like I was supposed to. I went to the optometrist to get my eyes checked. It all seemed normal and benign. I remember having my tonsils taken out at four (but I don't know how necessary that was; all I know is that they were killing me), so it seemed like a necessary procedure at the time. We received Polio vaccinations with the sugar cubes we ate, which also seemed reasonable at the time. I remember having my only vaccination for the bird flu or something over 50 years ago. I recall going to the fairgrounds and getting an injection when I was 10 or 11 (which was the first and only flu shot I ever received). I remember having the flu and going to the doctor at about age 9 or 10. He just looked at me and sent me home with instructions to take some aspirin. He left the room and my mom said to me, "Well, you hate being sick and hate sick people." Years later when I completed my Doctor of Chiropractic degree, she added the statement, "I can't believe you ever became a doctor."

The reality of going to school and listening to instructors in the 1970s talking about healthcare, talking about practicing medicine, how to treat patients, and what to do doesn't really prepare you for actually doing it! When I got out of school in 1980, I went to work for a doctor. I remember treating a lady with a stiff, sore neck I was supposed to treat her, it's what I had been *trained* to do. I vividly remember that I actually panicked, walked out of the room, found the doctor, and asked if he could help me. I didn't know what to do with her. Reflecting on it years later, I began to see that the academicians that trained us struggled as well. Many were not practicing physicians it is classic "Do as I say, not as I do." They talked about how anatomy works (physiology) sharing small nuggets of 'wisdom' about what helps when working with patients. The reality comes when you are facing your first patient, that's where the rubber really meets the road! I didn't have enough experience to even know when or how to decide which tool I should use, or what to say to patients. We learn as we go, I guess that's why they call it practicing!

Through the years I've had some patients that scared me. Cancer patients were the worst ones for me because I did not know what to say to them. In school, doctors are taught that they were going to fix everybody. In other words, everybody is going to get well, and everything is going to be fine. But the reality is that everybody is going to die. It's a matter of when, not if. The only question is what kind of health they are in when they do meet their end. It is the sad reality; it is the truth. How you approach health is what makes the difference with your patients.

I graduated chiropractic college in 1980. My practice consisted of chiropractic care with almost no nutritional component. I was a skilled adjuster and started adjusting people building a successful practice. I would see 75 people a day, worked five and a half days a week, and my patients were happy. They were adjusted and felt good. I remember buying health insurance for my whole staff back then. It was like $35 to $40 per person for insurance policies with a $200 deductible, making it easy to insure my staff.

Vaccinations were not yet in vogue then, and there was no real push for the flu shot. While they were available during the season, people seemed generally healthy. As we went into the late 1980s, people were noticeably sicker. Some of the things that started showing up were diabetes, hypertension started becoming more common place. From there it was a snowball effect. I watch this evolve, still not realizing the major shift in Western Medicine. We weren't seeing a lot of hip or knee replacements yet and people did not have those issues as much as today. Back surgeries, when performed were generally disasters, screwing up more people than they helped. Therefore, chiropractic was a good option.

As the 1990s rolled around, insurance premiums started doubling and tripling. A policy that used to be $35, was now $200, and insurance coverage for chiropractic care dropped off dramatically from what it was in the 1980s. We saw more information creeping in about diabetes and alcoholism treatment. What got my attention was that the definitions and classifications had changed. I decided it would be prudent to take out some disability insurance for myself in case I became sick or was injured, my office would be covered. During the interview I talked to the gentleman for an hour, during the interview he asked me the question. "How many alcoholic drinks do you have a day?" I asked why and what the indicators were. He told me that if you had three alcoholic drinks a day or more, you actually qualified as an alcoholic, and the insurance policy would allow treatment for you because you met the definition of being an alcoholic. Looking at it now, I realize the absurdity of diagnosing a disease based on something that simplistic with no other history or indications to support the premise. But it taught me an important lesson about definitions and about the direction health care was going.

What does your blood sugar have to be at to be called a diabetic? We saw those threshold numbers starting to drop, so more people qualified as diabetic. Then we saw the fact that if you qualified for those designations, insurance started to cost more money. In other words, if your blood sugar was a certain level, your file was stamped DIABETIC and you paid more for insurance. Or if you were an alcoholic, your file was stamped with that title and you paid more. If you had hypertension or high blood pressure, the numbers changed, and you were labeled at risk for that. Categorization became prevalent, forcing people to be labeled and grouped, targeting them for higher insurance premiums or disqualifying them for having "preexisting conditions," all with the sole purpose of raising insurance premiums.

Next came the pharmaceutical revolution multiple different blood pressure medications kept evolving dramatically, each being touted as being better than the one before. There was a surge in the push to vaccinate, and flu shots came into vogue. During the early 2000s, we saw the arrival of a whole new genre of medication. Statin drugs "the be all and end all" for those who had or might be at risk of developing high cholesterol. When I was in school, I remember having an instructor who was extremely sharp on cholesterol. I remember him telling me that he had decided to take all the cholesterol out of his diet. Instead, of curing his high cholesterol he ended up in the hospital with hypercholesterolemia because his liver had been forced to produce the cholesterol he wasn't getting. Cholesterol is produced in the liver. Can it become a problem? Yes. Yet medication should never be the first line of defense for addressing the issue. We had seen autopsies from the 20-year-old kids coming back from Vietnam, showing plaque in the arteries. This is where the "why of why" I spoke about in an earlier chapter becomes critical.

In my opinion, this is where healthcare started to struggle. There was a gradual shift in treatment methodology. The Pritikin diet came out about this time as a guide on how we should eat. That was one of the original dietary changes meant to address cholesterol and heart disease. There were some mistakes in what he did, but it was a start. But on the other side—I will call it the dark side of Western medicine—things were rapidly trending towards a drug culture treatment. In other words, you take cholesterol medications, you take diabetic medication, you take blood pressure medication, you get your flu shots, and you get your other immunizations.

The one that really got my attention in a big way was Celebrex which debuted in the 1990s. This was a NSAID (non-steroidal anti-inflammatory) that sky-rocketed to popularity for arthritis pain. Many people reported gaining much relief from this drug. I remember a patient who came into my office with knee and hip pain. I treated her back because that is what I did 30 years ago. I had no tools and we only did simple dietary treatments, adding only a few supplements back then. She stated she was taking Celebrex and said, "My hip pain and knee pain are totally gone. I feel wonderful." Guess what? In a year and a half, she was having her knee and hip joints replaced. Today we know that Celebrex may cause heart issues, but it definitely stops your own stem cells from reproducing. If you have a knee or hip injury, Celebrex stops your stem cells from reproducing and creating healthy tissue. All the drug does is it eats away at your joint and within a couple of years, you have no joint left. It was a real eye-opener to see that play out. At that time, I did not totally understand it, looking back knowing what I know now it is tragically clear. Twenty-twenty hindsight, as they say.

I have watched mainstream medicine go down this pharmaceutical pathway for many years now, funding medical schools teaching only pharmaceutical based protocols. They have slowly infiltrated naturopathic colleges, subverting them the same way they did the DO's (Doctors of Osteopathy) in the1970s. They were offered the opportunity to have a broader scope of practice performing surgeries if they prescribed more drugs, and they would be covered by insurance. The pharmaceutical companies are exceptionally good at dangling the "carrot." There are rumors currently that one of the drug companies is buying a naturopathic college in Seattle. The drug company is basically training naturopaths to be more allopathic drug-oriented doctors. This has already happened in Arizona where naturopaths have been tasked with stemming the tide of opioid dependence that has devastated many in our country. Conveniently the drug companies now have a drug to treat drug addiction. Definitely a 'win-win' for someone.

I have watched these shifts for many years and two things I see clearly are that we can no longer afford healthcare, let alone treatment, and that we have stopped treating disease. We now treat symptoms of disease with a plethora of pills in every size, shape, and color. Yet no one seems to get better. The only thing they get is farther in debt, more pills, and they get sicker. The question we need to ask is, "Is this truly healthcare?" And more importantly, is this where we want to go? Why don't we treat the causes of all these problems instead? What is the cause of the cancer? What is the cause of diabetes? What is the cause of high blood pressure? I am asking about the why of the why.

In the last 10 years our whole direction of treatment has changed. A patient will say to a doctor, "I am overweight, don't feel good, and my liver is going bad." Okay, what is this patient being told? "Well, you've got cirrhosis of the liver." Well, does this patient ever wonder why they have cirrhosis? "Well, I drank for 20 years." Okay, we know the patient has burned their liver out. In Western medicine, there is not much treatment for that. You can take anti-inflammatories to reduce inflammation, try managing other symptoms with drugs which in turn put more stress on the liver, or we can try and rebuild the liver. Eating foods that support and heal, maybe some herbal supplements. We go to the whys behind the conditions.

The challenge becomes this; a patient that comes for treatment, they are paying maybe $600 or $800 a month for "health" insurance and have a $2,000 to $10,000 deductible. They have no money left to even come into my office. They want their insurance to cover their treatment, but insurance does not cover "healthcare." Insurance covers if you break your arm, have a stab wound, or are in an accident. If you need a drug, insurance will cover that (but only if your insurance company's formulary covers it). Health insurance has nothing to do with "healthcare."

A paradigm shift must occur. When I hear political arguments about, "We need health insurance for all," nobody has health insurance in this country. You have sick insurance; it does not cover healthcare.

I had a lady come in five years ago in December 2015. We can call her Ann. Ann came in and had been treated for breast cancer in July. Her specialists did chemotherapy, a double mastectomy, and she went through radiation for six weeks. At the end of her treatment her doctor said, "Your cancer is gone. You're fine! Go live your life. You're out of here." In September of that year, she started feeling pain in her right hip. In October, she received a cortisone shot in the hip. Ann said receiving the shot was brutally painful, did not help, and just made her pain worse. She felt horrible. In November, she had X-rays done and found out she had bone cancer all through her body. Ann went in to consult with her medical doctor and he looked at her and said, "There's nothing I can do for you. You can leave now." She came into my office in December asking what I could do. I said, "I can make you feel better. We can get you functioning, out of pain, and maybe help you," because no one would see Ann or even treat her. We gave her a course of nutrient IVs. She felt better, yet she died within two months—but she was not in pain. Did I do my job? Yes. She had been abandoned by the very system she'd bet her life on.

I had another lady come in with unbelievably bad rheumatoid arthritis, extremities twisted and deformed. She had been treating for 13 years with a rheumatologist and was given chemotherapy and other drug interventions to stop the arthritis. After 13 years of treatments she is then told "We can't help you anymore. You need to leave." She asked, "Well, can I try some natural remedies?" Her doctor replied, "You can do that, but it will not help you. But you can just leave." I found out later that the same doctor was on one of the pharmaceutical boards and wanted no alternative care, only mainstream medicine. He basically crippled her after 13 years of chemotherapy and the arthritis drugs he had prescribed. Again, we helped relieve her pain and were successful in that.

People with Stage 4 cancer are probably the most challenging. Sadly, these cases are the epitome of our failed healthcare system. I have many people come in who have been through chemotherapy, have no immune system left, no energy left, at that point all that can be done is to give them truth and make them comfortable. I have learned that those simple things can be a great gift to the patient and their loved ones. I feel blessed to be able to give that to patients. I mean, who are you going to stop from dying? Everybody is going to die. If you could make the transition easier, give them more energy so they feel better, and can enjoy the time they have left, it's the best you can do.

We had a poor lady in her 80s who had been through everything, and her family carried her into the office refusing to accept that she was dying. They all stood around her in the room in the back of the office. We did nutrition IVs which gave her enough energy so she could visit with her family and say goodbye to them. She died later that day, but I felt good and the family thanked me for making her more comfortable so she could have those final few minutes with them. It makes you feel good to provide a service that nobody else will. We have a system where a doctor can kick a patient out of the office and say, "We can't help you." Often making it seen that the patient has somehow failed the doctor and is responsible for the treatment failing.

It goes back to what your job *really is* in healthcare. Mine is quality of life with the least amount of effort, the least risk, cost, and the best results. It doesn't mean that patients aren't going to die. Maybe they will live longer and healthier, maybe not. Ideally, they will be in less pain. We see patients all the time in my office who want to be 20 years old again. A patient may be 60 and say, "Well, I could do this when I was 20," but then I remind them of their actual age. When you get to this stage in life, the reality is your stem cells are not producing at the same rate they did when you were 20. You are not producing nearly as many healthy cells as the rate of cells dying every day. (Basically, more cells are dying than are being made.) This is truly the aging process. We look at ways of turning that around.

This speaks to the whole system of what it costs us to do what we are doing. We do not really have healthcare in this country, we have symptom treatment and trauma care. My definition of healthcare is preventatively treating the body to have the best quality of life possible for the longest period of time. Our system is more about treating your pocketbook and what your insurance covers.

I had the President of Regence Blue Cross come up to my office about eight years ago. Sitting there, he was so mad that he was shaking. I'd had the opportunity to testify in U.S. Senate hearings on healthcare, and I was blunt about what I said. He said, "Quit talking bad about us," and I said, "When you quit being an [____] to everybody, then I'll quit talking bad about you." I continued, "You don't do doctors any good and you don't do patients any good. You have nurses dictating what care a patient gets. You have limited coverage for what a doctor can do when there are procedures in healthcare that can help people you do not allow them to be covered."

Here is an example that I've given to the senators' offices I have been working with. If we take 100 bad knees that are currently being treated by surgical intervention at a cost of roughly $50,000 per knee, we will have a price tag of about $5,000,000. This does not include therapy or time off from work, which would increase numbers. By using alternative treatments that are less expensive, less invasive, less painful and require little to no rehab time, conservatively we could keep 50% of those knees from ever needing replacement. For a hundred patients, it would cost less, much less than $200,000. It would save $2.3 million.

People say, "Well, why don't you tell the insurance companies? Oh my gosh, this would be amazing to save that money!" The insurance companies do not care. You could get into technicalities and split hairs on this, but if they have higher premiums, they have more profits, and stockholders make more money. They really do not care about what is effective—and I'm talking most insurance companies, maybe not all of them. But most are interested in the bottom line of what they end up getting for profits at the end of the day and what the stockholders receive in profits.

When we instituted the Meaningful Use program, efficiencies of chiropractic offices dropped by 30%. Chiropractors saw fewer people because they did not have time to fit them all in as before. Looking at a computer screen takes away the ability to treat the patient. If boxes are not filled in, you do not get paid. I went to a cash-only practice years ago because I gave up on the whole system. I was not going to play the game anymore, which is why the President of Regents Blue Cross was so mad at me, because he had no noose around my neck anymore. I did not have a contract with him. He asked if I would sign a contract and I refused. I told him, "If you start taking care of doctors and patients, I'll talk to you. Otherwise, don't even talk to me." It felt really good to be able to say that.

As I said before, the dilemma is treating patients who are insurance poor. We need to change the system! Years ago, I looked at and worked with congressional offices about building health co-ops. The premise was to take 200 to 400 people, provide a medical doctor, a chiropractor, and a naturopath. These practitioners would do bloodwork, consultations on diet and nutrition, treat musculoskeletal conditions (not quite to the point of surgery) for a monthly membership fee. Patients would pay wholesale prices for all services thereafter. I provide services that cost literally cents on the dollar. So rather than $200. for an injection, you would pay only the actual cost of the supplies used, a few dollars rather than the $200 fee that is presently charged. The goal of people that come in to receive these services is they would start out with a health plan that we would evaluate, do basic bloodwork, and have a goal within a year to reach. Maybe it is to quit smoking. Cut down on drinking. Drop cholesterol levels. Reduce weight. Start an exercise program. It would be conservative measures to make you healthier. By doing that, your group would pay obviously less money and the doctors would have a set group of patients, so they are not spending a huge amount of money to bill insurance companies. The services provided would be a true prevention program.

Is that really possible? Unfortunately, people have been conditioned to expect a doctor to heal them with no help from the patient themselves. I tell people all the time, "I cannot heal you. You are responsible for healing yourself. I will work with you; we can work together as a team, but you have to realize you're ultimately responsible for your health." Our healthcare system fostered the idea and patients have bought into the idea that there is a magic pill for everything. You can do whatever you like and there will be a pill to cure what ails you. Traditional medicine took the expectation of personal responsibility and gave it to a pill. That is the last thing that is going to heal someone. You must take responsibility for your health!

When I started chiropractic college, I was paying $500 a quarter in school in the late 70s. By the time I was graduating, it was $800 a quarter. Medicare reimbursement was $14 per visit in 1980–81. Now, 40 years later, Medicare pays $32 and the cost of school today is $10,000 a quarter. Our system is completely out of proportion when you look at education versus reimbursement. How many patients would you have to see at $32 each to pay back a $100,000 student loan? That doesn't figure office overhead, wages, software, or anything else.

When I began my practice, we had paper billing and services

we billed insurance for were covered by a handful of billing codes. We were reimbursed by insurance, the patient paid what wasn't covered. We had no major computer systems or software to deal with. We did not have to have a full time IT person, and we didn't need extra employees to handle insurance billing. Today my overhead, has increased by 300%. Not only do we have the $32 Medicare reimbursement, but we also have an overhead that used to be 20% and is now up to 60%. Doctors today have student loans of $300,000 and are paying $1,400 each month on them. They cannot afford to start their own practices and are forced into this corporate medicine model, which is another reason why we are seeing hospitals buy practices. I have seen many demographic changes in my years in practice, I can honestly say not many have been positive and the vast majority have not improved patient outcomes at all!

People site Obamacare when discussing the failure of our system, when in reality things went south with a system brought in with one of the recovery plans 11 years ago. It was a plan called Meaningful Use, which was supposed to stop drug misuse. There was *one sentence* in the bailout package from the financial crisis of 2008 that *created 16 federal agencies underneath that plan.* The government built a computer program that when ideally used, doctors could enter all the drugs the patient took, it would go to a database, and would indicate a red flag if patients were overusing drugs or if one drug was contraindicated with what they were currently taking. The program would allow you to consult the patient on drugs they should not be taking or bad drug interactions. This program also paid $44,000 to every doctor that decided to incorporate this software into their system. It failed miserably. It never worked, yet we still have those 16 agencies in place today. Meaningful Use increased documentation requirements 10-fold for doctors and staff . We still have the documentation requirements which have been adopted by all insurance companies not just Medicare. If doctors did not buy into this system, they would be fined 3-5% on their Medicare reimbursement each year. The program has necessitated dramatic increases in office overhead to employ enough staff to implement and run the program, making it difficult to run a private practice.

You are left with little choice other than to go into corporate medicine with drug driven protocols.

Next, we look at ICD-9 coding systems. These are alphanumeric codes that are used to allow us to bill insurance companies for services provided. Chiropractors had 16, ICD-9 codes among literally thousands of codes in the ICD-9 coding manual, that covered our services—mainly spinal adjustments. They did not cover nutrition, exams, or X-rays. Then, came ICD-10 which was designed *"to provide greater specificity in diagnosis to provide more accurate reimbursement."* In reality it gave us 256 codes which has made no appreciable difference to reimbursement, increased office overhead and staff to deal with this unwieldly dinosaur.

To really appreciate the trouble, we are in we need to compare the cost of insurance, the deductible, and the cost of healthcare left to pay after insurance with the care we are getting. Do you feel like your care has increased as exponentially as the cost of services? From where I sit, I can tell you that office overhead continues to rise along with insurance premiums, more time is spent documenting, less time is spent interacting with patients, yet quality of care has changed very little. I hear from so many patients how they go to their doctor and when explaining things to their doctor, he or she is on the computer the entire time, not responding to the patient. Where has our healthcare system gone? We have limited services in some areas. We have definitions driving services with no interest in you as a patient. You do this, then you jump through this hoop, then you jump through that hoop, then we do surgery. Or we do chemotherapy, we do this, we can put you on these drugs (which we know cause their own problems). The trickle-down effect seems to be just rolling us into a system that is not healthcare at all, it is drug management.

Our local hospital decided they wanted to make Orofino; a town of 3,000 people, a "destination site for healthcare." I thought it was an interesting proposition. At their meeting were physical therapists from town, I was there, other hospital employees and even Representatives from the Chamber of Commerce were present. The hospital wanted to make Orofino a model for healthcare. I listened to them talk for a while and eventually I said: "Okay, let's talk business. What is healthcare? Your idea of healthcare is a colonoscopy and a mammogram. We know that colonoscopies now cost upwards of $3,500 and can result in trauma and damage to a lot of patients. We know a stool sample will catch most any colon issue before a colonoscopy would become necessary. Ninety percent of them do not even need to be performed. But that's healthcare. That is $3,500 that someone pays (or insurance covers). This does not include treatment; it is a test. The mammograms are a test. We are not preventing breast cancer. Where really is your healthcare? If you have cholesterol problems, you get cholesterol drugs. If you have high blood pressure, you get blood pressure drugs. If you have diabetes, you get diabetes drugs. When do we do healthcare?" They just looked at me and went, "Oh," and it was the last meeting we had on that venture.

We had two individual medical practices and the Hospital Clinic in Orofino when I first moved here. The private clinics did a good job with patients. These were old-time medical doctors. They really sat down with each patient and saw a fair number of patients, 30 to 50 in a day. Those clinics have been sucked up by Corporate Medicine.

The medical doctor in the corporate hospital only saw 13 to 15 people all day at the clinic. With that few patients, they have to produce a lot of money from each visit. A lot of that time during a patient visit goes to documentation. Let's see… you wait for an hour or so in the reception room, wait for an hour in the room, the doctor comes in for five minutes (documenting all this time), and then he or she is gone. This speaks to a couple of things, one of which is standard of care.

One of my sideline pursuits for the past 30 years is doing medical malpractice work. I am one of the top people in the Northwestern United States for these cases. One of my areas of expertise is standard of care. Standard of care means if you take five doctors of any specialty (chiropractor, medical doctor, etc.) in a region (such as a county), there would be a standard way they treat a patient for a certain condition. The standard would be that if someone came in with high cholesterol, there is certain bloodwork you would run, a certain amount of time spent with the patient, and medications you would prescribe. That is the standard of care. If a doctor were to talk to the patient about nutrition, he would fall outside the standard of care. It is frowned upon for doctors to do that, so they cannot practice outside the standard of care. Otherwise, their license would be threatened.

Say you have a group of chiropractors and they all do a basic exam on a stiff neck. If they do less than the basic exam and then adjust the patient, they have fallen below the standard of care. You could do more without an issue, but there is a basic protocol of things that need to be done. The medical doctor with a high cholesterol patient is bound by the same thing. There is a circle of protocols they must do, and one of them is to actually discuss available drugs with the patient. But what if the doctor also discussed nutrition? The problem is that if the doctor already discussed available drugs, they would not (or could not) discuss alternative modalities. Some clinics forbid any mention of alternative therapies. I know some groups will not allow their doctors to do any alternative care at all; they must stay strictly with the mainstream medical guidelines. If you go to a medical group that is owned by a hospital, I will guarantee you their standard of care is pretty much mainstream medicine. Standard of care is what drives the whole system.

This is where we run into issues with insurance companies. I had a lady experiencing severe back pain, from a herniated disc, we knew it was a problem. I told her to see her MD and have an MRI done. She did that, the doctor prescribed an MRI for her, it was authorized by the insurance company (Blue Cross), and she had it done. Later they said, "We didn't authorize that., so you have to pay for it," so she had a $5,000 MRI to pay for that shows the herniated disc. We were able to treat it with conservative measures and saw improvement with ozone injections, but her standard of care was being determined by the insurance company.

If you come in with abdominal pain, what is the standard of care for that? You have bloodwork done, likely an ultrasound maybe and they find that your gallbladder is bad. Now there are other hoops that must be jumped through prior to surgery. All these hoops are to confirm medical necessity, on the surface this sounds entirely reasonable. The reality is surgery is always their first option, all the rest is just ways to get more money prior to the final outcome, surgery.

I had a patient who came in with breast cancer. She was getting worse and wanted to try some other therapies but was told point-blank that if she did anything alternative, they would make sure she was kicked off Medicare. That is a horrible prospect, but this is what is going on right now, and it's driven by the standard of care.

Then we hear about malpractice issues, which always amazes me. Statistically, over the course of their career, a doctor can have five to 15 lawsuits against them. This stems from poor communication with patients. I have had poor outcomes from patient treatments but have never been sued in my 40 years of practice.

Paul Harvey talks about two different styles of doctoring. One doctor spends time talking with his patients, taking the time to actually connect with them. The other a new hotshot doctor, runs services and pushes people through the system. The hotshot had been sued 15 times because he never talked to his patients, he never really listened to them. I think it is important for patients to be able to select their doctor. How do you even find a doctor anymore? I've heard of Medicare patients that when trying to find a medical doctor are being told by the offices that they no longer accept Medicare. They are told the paperwork is too much of a problem and reimbursement is a problem We have other people that are in these corporate medicine clinics and they are treated like a number. They do not get a doctor they see all the time they get whoever is on call or available. Selecting a doctor is challenging for people.

I get calls all the time because I train doctors in procedures that are cutting edge. People call me asking if I could get them in. I tell them, "Well, I can, but you should see someone in your area to follow up," and they are hard-pressed to find anybody. I do not know if it's personalized medicine or actually building a healthcare system (which is what it's going to take), but our present system is not going to do it. We need to eliminate soaring office overhead and the standard of care needs to be changed to a system that provides healthcare rather than pills. The federal requirements on documentation also need to change because that is 30% of the practice overhead that has nothing to do with improved patient care.

I think patients should approach a consultation more as an interview. You are interviewing a doctor to see if he will be a good fit for you. Doctors and patients alike seem to get stuck in this loop of feeling obligated to treat this patient or see this doctor, when the reality is that we all have choices. By not choosing this doctor it simply means he's not a good fit for you. By not treating this patient it simply means it's not a good fit. The goal is to choose the best fit. This should be our mindset at our first meeting. Does this doctor listen to me, is he willing to look at different options? Or is he primarily interested into fitting me into the box he's created. Is he willing to explore other options? Does he offer solutions that align with my needs, goals, and finances? Is he a dictator or a coach? It is hard because patients don't even know what questions to ask.

I love patients that come in with a stack of records three or four inches thick. They set them on my desk like this is the sum total of their life. I look at the stack, not opening the file and ask, "Why are you here today?" They look at me, not really sure what to do next. I ask again, "Why are you here today? What issue is concerning you right now?" There is a reality check that happens then. Many doctors will spend hours reviewing that pile of records. But really, you are treating the person not that stack of records. It is important sometimes to get a background, but in reality, you are treating the patient as they present here today, not as they've been the past 10 years!

I had a lady and her husband come in. She was in her 60s. She and her husband both were 40- or 50-pounds overweight. She said she had taken a blood test that said she had breast cancer and wanted me to treat her. The lady said, "The test said if I treat it with high-dose Vitamin C, it will help treat my cancer." Okay, that is fine, however she had not been to a medical doctor and didn't want to go, but she wanted to do a Vitamin C IV. I told her, "To treat this, you're not looking at just one dose of Vitamin C to fix your cancer. You are also looking at the fact that unless you change your lifestyle, your diet, get off the breads, the sugars, the wheats. All those things that feed cancer—you are not going to get better. You are looking at one or two treatments a week of high-dose Vitamin C for probably three to six months.

One treatment only is going to do nothing for you. Unless you are actively involved in the treatment, none of this serves any purpose for you. If you come back in a couple of weeks and have gotten rid of all these foods, then we'll talk." Of course, I did not see her again.

I get some interesting comments when I make recommendations to patients. "I can't quit my bread," or, "I can't quit my alcohol or cigarettes." Well, then how can I help you if you won't help yourself? When are you going to be responsible? If you are not going to take any responsibility, I can't help you. So how does that come across to a patient? I've had that discussion with several people. They have been everywhere else, they've spent tons of money and finally come to me, want one treatment, and think that one treatment from me is going to fix them. They are just asking for failure. I will not play that game with them. I cannot care more about your health than you do.

I think that the first step is to find a doctor you can spend 10 minutes with. If you cannot spend 10 minutes and figure out if that doctor is going to work for you, you are going to need to find another doctor. But the expectation must be that you are responsible for your health when you walk in. If you are not and you expect them to heal you, you're looking in the wrong spot. Nobody is going to do that for you. Our current symptom-based system will give you drugs, surgeries, and chemotherapy, with no resolution of the problem. Some people buy into this broken system wholeheartedly, and that is the problem. It is a normal route to take for a lot of people.

Want to know the difference between an allopathic doctor and a holistic doctor? Let's say you walk into their office with a sliver in your foot. If you go to the allopathic doctor and say that your foot hurts, you get pain medication. You will still have the sliver in your foot, but it won't hurt. If you go to a holistic doctor, he will take the sliver out, you are still going to have some pain, but the cause has been eliminated. Understand the choices you have.

When I teach my seminars, I treat doctors and other patients that I've never seen before and know nothing about. I have just moments to look at someone do a basic exam and then determine how to treat them. I never fail to gain a wealth of knowledge from that brief contact, but I will tell you it's taken years of practice to be able to do that.

When it comes to looking for a physician, learn to look deeper than the surface. Is this someone running through a system check like your auto mechanic you need an oil change and a new filter and you're out the door. Or is this someone who looks deeper, asks questions, and takes time to hear what you need?

Life is short. We only live one day at a time and it is important to get the full benefit of that in our experiences every day. Be present in the moment, that moment will never happen again!

Chapter 10

"One cannot think well, love well, sleep well, if one has not dined well!"

—Virginia Woolf

This speaks to the evolution of what we eat. After 40 years of being in practice and 45 years working with nutrition, I have seen many changes. I have been watching the evolution over time of what people have preached, done, and tried, using different supplements and programs. It started with Amway and Shaklee in the 1960s/1970s, changing again in the 1980s.

Currently, my wife and I just finished eight weeks of fasting. We stop eating on Sunday night and do not resume eating until Wednesday night. All we take in is magnesium, iodine, and trace minerals, and water. During that time we read a book on liver health. My wife had gestational diabetes when she had her daughter, so she had been on the cusp of diabetes forever. She exercised religiously and never had blood sugar issues. With our busy schedule exercise time diminished and blood sugars became a problem. Several years ago, while attempting to understand why morning blood sugars were always elevated beyond what food intake and fasting could account for, she had an adrenal ultrasound done. It came back normal; however, it was noted by the radiologist that there were the beginnings of a fatty liver.

My wife was quite put out by the idea that her liver was fat! Where does that come from? My wife is not overweight and works tirelessly to make sure she stays fit. She always had that stubborn five pounds that would disappear during our three-day fasts and gradually reappear a pound at a time once we started eating again. She rarely ate more than one meal a day which consisted of meat and a salad, a handful of nuts or some avocado slices, which were her daily normal. She decided to take the advice in the book *Liver Detox* by Anthony Williams and try to heal her liver.

We went from a heavily Keto type diet high in "healthy fats" to a very low-fat diet high in fruits and vegetables. When she was on a high fat diet, her blood sugar stayed more often within normal limits although she was still plagued by random unexplained highs seemingly unrelated to food intake. We were able to keep her blood sugar down, but is it the healthiest way to go? We are finding the way that her liver metabolizes fat, the fasting is actually harder on her liver. Some of the diets out there like the Code Red Diet, Carnivore, Keto and Atkins consists of heavy fat diets. This puts more stress on the liver. You can maintain the system, until it's too sick to maintain but you're not really doing the healthiest things for your body. Within a couple weeks of starting the *Liver Detox* book, she lost the stubborn five pounds plus five more besides that! All while consuming five times the amount of food I'd ever seen her eat! Her hormones changed dramatically as well.

In the evolution of the patient education classes we've done for the last couple of years, I have looked at the basic diet we give patients. We eliminate all the carbs, sugars, fruits with fats, and processed foods. We have been able to control diet, help cholesterol, reduce weight, help arthritis, and slow cancer, but are we really doing the best for patients? I find that 80% of people do great on the diet and the other 20%, it does not matter what you do with it, they don't lose weight or feel better. It makes you wonder why.

Last year, I was talking to patients and thinking of what drove me to nutrition in the first place. When I first moved here in the 1980s, I found out that we had (in my opinion) a high rate of cancer. When I checked closer, I found out we did not, but we did have cancer rates like the rest of the country. Interestingly, I learned that ranchers would give selenium shots to their cattle, so they would not develop white muscle disease—a type of cancer. Then I found out there is no naturally occurring selenium on this side of the Continental Divide. Unless you obtain selenium from another source, you would be deficient in it. Basically, if you have a lack of selenium, you have higher rates of cancer.

The other side of the Continental Divide, Nebraska through

the Mississippi river valley, has naturally occurring selenium. But what is the reason we don't have enough selenium? If you look at nutrition maps around the world, there are different areas that have selenium and others that do not. Our selenium sources used to be through anadromous (migrating) fish. Those are salmon that run up the river and die in the streams. Animals eat the carcasses or drink the water, pee in the woods, the selenium goes into the soil, and then into the plants. Animals that eat those plants have a selenium source. Since we have lost the amount of anadromous fish, we found out nutritionally that the system wasn't healthy, which translates to the human body. We are a vector that needs a vector of foods to feed our system and make our metabolism work.

Canadians have tested bore samplings of 400-year-old trees on the Pacific coast. They could tell you how big the salmon runs were by the amount of nitrogen and the growth of the rings that year. If you look nutritionally at that region and how we ate, we must take that into consideration. What has changed in the last 100 years with our diets? Access to foods. Let us take it a few steps farther and it will all make sense as we go on with this concept.

The Nez Perce Indians, which have been in this area for thousands of years, had diets of 95% fish. There were runs of fish that were in these rivers for 10 months out of the year, so the availability of fish was ever present. Realize that we are 700 river miles from the ocean in our area on the Clearwater River, their home. The influence of anadromous fish (steelhead, salmon, and eels) led to their survival. The tribes would take the fish and dry them, eat them, and that was their sustenance. They were not great farmers, eating little bits of roots and berries during the summer. We know that fish have all the trace minerals, healthy fats, proteins, chromium, and Vitamin A—all of the substances to keep you healthy. The tribe spent the majority of their time outdoors in the sun, so the Vitamin D level was there. You could see a system that worked very well.

What happened when they were introduced to European foods? They would have grains, sugars, and alcohol. So, what do we have now? A high rate of diabetes and alcoholism because the Native population could not process sugars and has a lack of nutrients If you have part Nez Perce Indian genetics in you, you are NOT going to tolerate sugars well. You are not going to tolerate alcohol either. You will experience all the health issues such as eye and nervous system problems that go along with diabetes.

Let us take it a step farther. Think of what regional genetics goes back to and let's go around the world. Visit the tribes in Panama. Did they eat many fats or fish? There were no anadromous fish there, but they would eat local fish. What grows year-round in Panama? Everything. You could do four crops of watermelon a year there because vegetables and fruits grow well all year. They would eat a diet that was high in carbohydrates and high nutrients because of the rain forest, including small amounts of proteins and fats. Did their body adapt to that? Yes, they did. If we go around the world and looked at the people with the highest longevity, they live in those kinds of climates. There are different jungle tribes of people over 100 years old and they're healthier than the rest of us.

Let us jump now to an extreme environment, like Alaska and the tribal Indians that lived there—Eskimos. I was up there caribou hunting and considered how they have evolved. They mainly ate fat. Ninety-five percent fats—not proteins, but fat. They will take scoops of pure fat and eat it. What is the other thing that would happen? There was little fruit at all, only a few berries for a month out of the year, but mainly fat and some protein. Also, they found that the Eskimo Indians are the only humans that can produce small amounts of Vitamin C. Humans cannot generally produce Vitamin C, but mammals can. Why is this? None of the foods they ate had Vitamin C, so their bodies had to produce it.

Now, let us take an Eskimo Indian and put them in Central America on a traditional diet. Take a Panamanian Indian and put them in Alaska. Do you think either will survive? It would kill both in months from liver and pancreatic dysfunction, cardiovascular disease, and plaquing. Let us take it by the latitude that we're at now in Europe (around the 45th Parallel) and look at the populations there. We look at the people who ate a lot of grains, fruits, vegetables, and fish which was prevalent 4,000 or 5,000 years ago. They did not eat a lot of fats.

Look at you and I now, many of us are Heinz 57. All of us have a little bit of this, a little bit of that, and when we do genetic testing, we find all these different genetic influences. It begs the question of why there are problems with diet. Why can a diet work for one and not someone else? Our genetic programming to metabolize foods is different.

What is the way you eat? What would traditionally work if you went back in time, and what has changed? We can go to the supermarket and buy raspberries, strawberries, apples, and pineapple year-round. That did not exist 100 years ago. What is stored in the root cellars? Potatoes, onions, dried foods, dried meats, and fats. We altered our diet during the year. If we want to eat to the seasons, let us think about that a little bit. We are in June now. What is freshly harvestable? We have our early crop vegetables; some fruits are coming into play right now (like blueberries). There are other berries that will go through September or October.

If we shift away from the fats and proteins and eat vegetables, that is going to clean our liver out, clean our system out, and balance our sugar metabolism again. If we go into the fall, let us eat some meats and the cold vegetables that are in season. We eat fats from January through March, and then into the spring we go more towards vegetables again that naturally occur with the seasons. Our body metabolism is not regulated by what Costco has in the produce department that they ship from all over the world. Another caveat that plays into this is trace minerals in the soils. Which ones are in the anadromous fish zones? Which ones are naturally occurring? What area do they come from, and where does that vector come from?

When you look at the heavy fat and protein diet, the liver goes to hell in some people and they end up in the hospital. For other people, it might kill them. If you put 10 people on the same diet, they will not all respond the same way. We need to rethink our food paradigms in a different way to be healthy, and I think we need to look more toward eating to the seasons, understanding our genetics, and I think we will find a healthier lifestyle.

The lesson now is to take control of your diet. You must evaluate finances and budget resources. It is not expensive to eat healthy you must eat smarter. You are ultimately the benefactor of healthy decisions made. We offer a free guide on the Harper Chiropractic website at https://www.harper-chiropractic.com/. Start today by writing down everything you eat and drink for the next seven days and examine what you can do to eat healthier.

Chapter 11

"Emotion is messy, contradictory, and true."

—*Nigella Lawson*

For years, I had thought that when I came home wound up at night, it was because of *my* emotions. What I found out recently is that all those years I was wound up, weren't from my emotions, but everybody else's emotions. During a class recently I had an unsettling experience. I put my hand on a lady's forehead what I felt there made my body vibrate horribly. I could see it in her eyes that something was not right, but I didn't dare say anything to her in front of the class. I thought how much that really rattled me. If I had not known what I was feeling, I would have gone on with her baggage in my trunk, not even realizing it. It is important to touch patients. What I mean is that touching a patient is to understand what they feel and why. This goes back to Ryke Geerd Hamer's work which theorizes that cancer begins as a result of some type of unresolved trauma. Emotional, physical, mental, or financial trauma that we have been unable to resolve. A cycle of pain that the brain is unable to disconnect from. It changes the energy of the body and can be felt.

Shirley and I have the pleasure of staying with our friends Bob and Katrina down in Orange whenever we are in LA. We have a true connection and are great friends. They would do anything for us, and we would do anything to help them. We met originally because Katrina suffered an injury which left her with longstanding health issues. It is fun to talk to them about energy medicine, the power of touch, what they felt at our first meeting and hear how relieved they felt to know that someone heard them and knew how they felt about what was going on. Those sentences are a mouthful and may take some thinking to digest. In short, it means that if you open up your feelings to yourself (the naked mirror test), you begin to sense other people's feelings and connections and relationships are much deeper, richer if you will.

Keith was my neighbor. He lived about a block away and I could see his house from my porch. We were best buddies growing up. We ran around and did everything together. We played on the dirt hill and had dirt clod fights. We went fishing; his dad and my grandpa were commercial fisherman. We would ride our bikes everywhere and had countless adventures every day—(with no helmets on)—and spend all day at the docks with our fishing poles and 25 cents' worth of bait.

What is interesting is that I had not seen Keith in 55 years. I discovered him on Facebook last year. We ended up staying with him on the way to my class reunion. I had invited him up to Orofino because I want to spend more time reconnecting and help him heal from 10 years of back pain, the result of a Work Comp injury. I said, "Keith, if you come up, I can fix your low back for you." Fortunately, he came up this year and I got him pain-free for the first time in 10 years. It was exciting to see that. Even more interesting was listening to him and finding out about what his goals were in life, what he had accomplished, his fears and why he had them, and how he felt about himself. We had long discussions every evening. When Keith first arrived, he spoke about, "Yeah, I have to give my kids this because I'm going to die. I'll be dead soon." I asked, "Why are you saying that?" He kind of looked at me and said, "It's going to happen."

He was also very much into driving his truck 100 miles an hour and doing things like bungee jumping. He had to have some sort of adrenaline rush to make his life feel full. Keith would also exaggerate to get peoples' attention and sensationalize things. "I do this. I do that." Yet what drives that decision point? What was missing in his life that forced him to fill it with all that high energy stimulation? He was busy doing 'fun' things minus the happiness that should accompany them.

I look at mountain climbers that climb Mt. Everest. This looks like pure torture to me; I think it's absolutely nuts. What makes people do that? Is it self-worth? Is it that you never give yourself permission to be yourself? I really wanted to understand Keith. He said to me, "Well, I've been married four times." His wife would be riding along asking Keith, "Why don't you talk?" "Well, I was driving," Keith would respond. However, I couldn't shut him up the entire week he was there visiting with us. I think what it came down to is I gave him permission to be himself without any judgement.

So many times, we're afraid to talk or to be ourselves because someone will judge us. When someone has judged us harshly some time in our life, that makes us feel uncomfortable voicing our opinion. Instead, we sensationalize, use cuss words, or add some exaggeration. Anything to keep people at a safe distance from our true selves. Those fears are little voices that stay with us all the time. With that said, it was great talking to him. I said, "Keith, what you do is you give yourself permission to change your life a little bit at a time. Walk 15 minutes a day. Get some time to really talk to yourself about yourself. Get to know yourself again. Why do you have those fears? Why do you need that excitement? Why do you feel the need to drive fast? Is it a need or is it something fun to do? (I can see both sides of it.) But if it is something that drives you to, artificially replace something you should have, shouldn't you basically be able to sort those two things out and decide which it is?" That sounds confusing, but it comes down to the fact that ultimately you oversee your life.

Somewhere along the line his dad pushed him hard, and I think we see that from our families. Take those pieces apart to find why you have a fear of something. You know, I have a fear of bees. I have a fear of dogs. They came from an instant that happened that helped make me who I am today. Sometimes, it is a small incident. I used to love dogs. I went to my grandparents' place, which was right by Keith's house. I walked into the backyard and there was this big dog that weighed 110 pounds. He jumped up on my shoulders and ripped my shirt at the elbow. I have been petrified of dogs since then. Strange dogs come up to me and I am petrified. I recognize where it came from.

Then there is my fear of bees. I hate them! I was not afraid of bees when I was young. It was Keith, Ricky, and I playing by the house where the city had dug fresh ditches in front of my home. There was a hole in the ground and yellow jackets were coming in and out of it. We thought, "Well, that's fun. Let's plug the hole up!" We were six years old. Keith was across the ditch watching while Ricky and I were on the other side. We were all throwing rocks into this nest of bees. Well, guess what happened? Bees swarmed out of the hole and flew at Ricky and me. We took off running down the street while Keith was sitting there laughing. He did not move, so the bees didn't bother him. The bees were all following us. I looked over at Ricky as we were both crying and running down the street. He had a hole in his pants right below his crotch and a stream of bees were going up through that hole. I still have such a vivid memory of witnessing that. My dad heard us screaming and came running after us. He finally caught up to us and carried me back home. He took my clothes off and I had been stung maybe six or eight times. Ever since then when we go camping, if there is one bee, I am fine. Two bees, I throw my plate in the air and I run for cover. That's the way it was when I was younger. I have been absolutely petrified of bees ever since. It is part of me, and I understand it.

How many times do we have those incidents in life? For instance, we try to impress our dad and do something well. We may have come up short on it and we get chewed out, and suddenly, we are petrified to attempt that project again. Whether it is tying our shoes or riding a bike, maybe we do not do things fast enough, so we've got to do them faster. I was listening to Keith as he spoke about how his dad made him come out on the commercial fishing boat when he was younger. Well, he would get seasick. For a year and a half, Keith was seasick every time they went out. He puked his guts out every time his dad made him go out on the boat. He went every day during the summer. Every time he got seasick, his dad said, "You need to be faster at doing stuff." Is that where his 'go faster' thing came from? Now Keith must prove to himself that he can drive faster and go faster to prove to himself that he is somebody.

Like I said, I gave Keith the permission to talk. He was extremely comfortable and freely shared things. He did not quit talking every evening at the house. It was like a weight was lifted off his shoulders. I gave him permission to see the other side of who he was. We all need to look at who we really are sometimes and why we make the choices we do and the actions we take, asking, "Why do I really do this?" Why did Keith bungee jump? Was it just for fun or was it for adrenaline? It's not that it's a bad thing, but do we do it for the right reasons? What is the real reason behind why I am doing this? You do not have to overanalyze it, but just be realistic.

Growing up we go through lots of different steps. I finished the first three years of college and did my pre-chiropractic while still living at home. Moving to Portland Oregon in September 1977 to attend Western States Chiropractic College made me face responsibilities that were almost overwhelming. Now I take my life apart in pieces to look for the why.

I had interviewed with schools in Los Angeles and Portland. I felt that Portland was a better fit for me than Los Angeles. My folks bought a mobile home, which was awesome at the time. I would just pay space rent and at the end of my tenancy, they were able to sell the trailer for more money than the original purchase price. I rented the spare bedroom to another student from the school, which had its benefits and drawbacks—both with several disasters and learning curves. But it allowed me to live on my own and study, which was the important part.

My standard routine was to get up in the morning, go to class from 8 AM till 4PM, work until 11:30 or midnight every night, and study in between— When I was in school, I worked an average of 27 hours a week doing night jobs. I had a job at the store just down the block. It allowed me to study a couple of hours while I worked at a mini mart, which my boss was fine with. We were in class 34 hours a week; looking back, it was a horrendous schedule. My dad told me to pay for school as I went through it, so that is what I did. I almost paid for the entire thing but had to borrow $10,000 at the end. My student loan was $58 over the course of 10 years, which I paid off in time.

It was not a pace I wanted to keep forever. That was one of the times of setting a goal of getting out of college and being successful at it. Those decisions however, caused me to be out of balance in my life, shortsighted, pushing so hard with no idea of what balance was caused many things to happen that probably did not have to happen.

So, this is when things go bump in the night. We can drive

ourselves into a hole that takes years to dig out if we're lucky or maybe never get out. In our younger years we have so many rules which we're given by our parents, teachers, society, and even our own hormones. Hopefully, the hormones settle down as we get older, allowing us to have a little better focus. If you are under 25 and reading this book, think of what really drives you every day and every night. If you are over 25, look at why you have been driven to make the decisions, you made. I mean look at everything from profession/job, were you live, your spouse, the circle of friends you run with, and what kind of physical mental shape are you in. Time for the naked mirror test.

Chapter 12

"Time is precious, make sure you spend it with the right people."

—Unknown

This chapter speaks to the people you hang around with. It is interesting as we go along in life, to look at our relationships with others. How many times do you meet somebody and say, "Oh, they're my friend," or, "This person is my friend?" We loosely use that term all the time. When I moved to Lewiston in 1981, I got involved with the Metal Detecting and Prospecting Club and was one of the founding members. We panned for gold, looked for gems, and metal detected for artifacts or whatever we could find. In that group I met a gentleman named Bill. We started talking about metal detecting, hunting, and evolved into a relationship of doing many things together for the last 37 years. I look at our history and smile. We had several situations where he said, "Gee, Dennis. What are friends for?" and we would laugh about all the things "friends are for." I go back to thinking about that and I wonder what that comment is even about. With Bill, it was probably something different than I have with a lot of other people.

When I was at a seminar, I learned that the definition of a friend is somebody you could call at 2:00 in the morning, ask them for $5,000, and they'd write a check without even asking you why. I thought about that for years afterwards and my daughter asked me one time about what the definition of a friend is. I told her, "A friend is somebody you could call at 2:00 in the morning, ask them for $5,000, but realize a true friend would never ask that of you."

If you go back and define in your life what friends are for, what is a friend? I go back to Bill. We were sitting on top of a mountain, soaking wet from walking all day through the rain because Bill wanted to go to the top of the mountain, and I followed him. Looking at that, you think about relationships and who did this or that with you. To define it, you have got to go through stories, events, and ideas.

Bill had picked out a hike he had wanted to do. It happened to be at a place called The Nub. It was a 5,500-foot vertical climb in five miles up the hill, 10 miles total. My wife at the time asked, "Why are you doing that?" I said, "Because Bill wants to do it. That's what friends are for." You take those kinds of things and just do it. She replied, "Well, what if Bill wanted to go off the cliff?" I answered, "Well, I'd go right with him if he wanted to go, because that's what friends do."

We started our hike but never made it to the top of the hill. Bill's wife at the time came with us, slowing our ascent and we never made it to the top of the hill. We had hiked from 6:00 in the morning until noon and had put a deadline of noon to stop hiking. It was hot that day we were sweating like mad. My knee hurt so bad that coming down I had to slide over the bank, down the hill, and off the trail. I could barely walk the next day. Bill had wanted to do the hike, so we did, and I never questioned him. The beer sure tasted good when we got to the creek to cool off.

We did many hikes like that over the years, going to different places and doing different things. We always laughed, "Oh, what are friends for?" We were on a hillside cutting a log and Bill had me back up a little bit, back up a little bit more, and I slid 20 feet off a hill. I was laughing like, "Okay, what are friends for? To help push you over the side of the hill." We laughed about it for years.

There are so many times when I would get phone calls from patients saying, "Well, you're a friend of mine. Can you loan me some money?" That was an interesting thing to deal with, and I would have to say no. It just was not right. Going through life and looking at friends and relationships, it goes back to what we were talking about before. If you can truly give 100% and not expect anything in return, that is probably the best friendship if it works both ways. How many times do you have people who want to be your friend because they want something from you, or you could do something for them? It could be something random that does not have anything to do with being your friend.

Over the last 12 years I have trained at least 300 doctors on advanced procedures with injectables and stem cell products. We have a set of products, and specific protocols that consistently produce great outcomes. I had a doctor call he has attended several of our trainings over the last five to six years. He has never put into practice any of the things I've taught him. He uses none of the products we use, yet about once a year he calls me to tell me about some big venture he has in the works. He tries to cut corners on every item he can. Thus, he does not get the results he desires. He called me to get information at no charge when he does not use any of our products. He came to me to solve a problem for him. He wanted something for nothing. There comes a time when you say, "I am sorry, but I can't help you." He sounded like my best buddy on the phone, but he wanted everything for nothing.

In your relationship with your spouse, I feel it is probably the best to have a friendship first. I see many couples that have grown in different directions losing the friendship portion, or never really having it to begin with. It is also interesting how the relationship with your spouse can intertwine with other relationships and couples. When I was in the beginning stage of divorcing my ex-wife five years ago, I had what I believed was my best friend storm into my office, demanding I fix my relationship. He was sincere about wanting me to mend fences with her, but not because he cared about me, or her and I. His reasons were quite different indeed! He wanted the relationship with my ex-spouse and I to exist because it benefitted him. He did not care that I was unhappy he was concerned because it would affect our interaction as couples. Never once did he come to me and say, "Let's talk about this, is there anything I can do to help?" He was only concerned about himself, and we still do not talk to this day.

It is time now to ask yourself some questions about the "friends" you have in your life. Are they the anchor on your tail or the wind in your sail? If they are an anchor, gracefully find a way to exit or minimize your relationship, if they are the wind then nurture, appreciate, and be thankful for them!

Chapter 13

"Reality is merely an illusion, albeit a real persistent one."

—*Albert Einstein*

We finished our Idaho primary election Tuesday night 2020, which I lost. I am surprisingly happy I lost. The enormity of winning at this particular time in my life would have been overwhelming! I learned a tremendous amount and will likely run again in two years. I will be in a better position mentally at least, knowing now what the reality looks like. Until you open that door you just can't know what is on the other side. I served in the Idaho State Senate in 2007, filling in for another senator for a brief time. It provided me with a little bit of exposure to the position. But now the playing field has changed. The picture in politics with, the radicals on both sides (right and left)—oh, my God. How do you even deal with everything that comes with the job? Someone said this morning, "You would be honored by one side and seen as evil to the other side. It doesn't matter what, you're going to make somebody angry." You must mentally be ready to deal with it. It is just timing; I had in my mind when I started to campaign in February that is was my time. Now I am happy I lost the race. Perspective changes the tone of the entire situation.

It is often easy to look at doing a different job, maybe be a banker, a realtor, or whatever it may be, sitting on the outside it's interesting to look at a job and judge if it would be easy or hard, fun, or boring. Actually, making that a reality may be quite different than what you expected it would be

Creating Your Reality—What is your reality?

I remember reading books by Deepak Chopra and several different authors, talking about standing there and seeing a tree. The question is this: is the tree there or not? Is it an aberration of something else manifested as a tree, or is it in fact a tree? What type of tree would you see, what would be your perception? When we look at life and the direction we are moving in, ideally, we strive to create balance, getting all the right signals to react to "our tree" (metaphorically speaking).

When I started this journey toward my political aspirations six months ago, I framed things into what my perception of reality thought they would be. If you run for a political position, what do you do? We had many plans going into the campaign, plans to go places, meet people, etc. none of those things became a reality. With Covid came a drastic reality shift. So, our perception came nowhere close to what became our reality. We can never fully know the reality until it becomes reality. We must be honest with ourselves about that.

I went into the political arena realizing that I was going to get a lot of questions to start with, so I started fielding phone calls and having many conversations. "Oh, you're running against this person. Why are you running? What do you expect to get out of running? Do you have a vested interest as to why you are running? What's your reasoning and what are your expectations for what you're doing?" With that whole litany of questions, I was sent into a spiral of trying to balance everyone's expectations and still be honest with myself and true to my beliefs in the process.

When you look at the expectations of people when they come at you, they are looking at a tree differently than you do. You may look at a tree with five branches; they see a tree with 12 branches—or no branches at all, but they want you to see the tree as they do. To give an example, I met with a group of well-intentioned people that had a whole list of questions for me. There was a bill being contemplated in Idaho that would make it a felony with jailtime for a woman who had an abortion. Their belief is that abortion is wrong (which I agree with). That is the premise and the "tree." They are also opposed to raising taxes.

My question to them was twofold. One, why do we have a woman in a position that she needs to consider abortion? Two, what happens when we put her in jail? Who is going to pay for that? Once you have a felony conviction, you cannot apply for certain levels of jobs, so now they are going to be on the tax rolls forever—you've virtually destroyed that woman's life. So how are you justifying paying for that without raising taxes? Who is going to pay it? Who is going to be responsible for that? Of course, there was silence. What they wanted to hear was, "Oh, yeah. Let's throw them in jail! Let's give 'em hell!" I said, "No."

Why not go back to the cause (which we've talked about before). What are we looking at? The end result is a woman who got pregnant. Probably unintentionally, but why? Probably a lack of education, self-esteem. Maybe it was a situation she should not have been in. It could be that she was not being responsible, because she did not understand what her responsibility was. Why not go back and teach people responsibility and educate them better, so they do not subject themselves to a situation where pregnancy is the end result. You are only treating the symptom by putting a woman in jail for procuring an abortion.

Let us look at the reality of the "tree." What reality do you expect out of the action you are taking, and are you thinking far enough back to create a solution, or are you just treating a symptom? The symptom is that you got pregnant and for some reason feel like you cannot have the baby. That is the symptom, not the cause of the situation. Let's take that back farther and rebuild that "tree," making the reality different for them.

I went through this whole election process with the reality thing on my mind, talking with different people who have special interests. In one instance, I received a note that was purely on the environment. "What are you going to do with global warming?" We are going to do things that make sense. I am going to look at facts and then make decisions based on those facts. We must balance everything to create a balanced environment. But I am not going to put corporations in jail and do this and that without deciding what can be done better and educating people about what we can do better. We come back to the point of creating a reality. My wife and I talked a lot about decisions legislators have to make and how little voters really understand about all the things that must be considered when making those decisions.

The public gets a brief snippet of a bill up for vote; example "getting rid of common core math" in our schools. Well who isn't for that!? What the public didn't see was that to do that

Idaho would have to relinquish millions of dollars in Federal aid immediately. Legislators voting against "getting rid of common core" were vilified in public with no concept of the reality of the situation, merely the perception of reality. What I gained during this process was the ability to use my natural predilection to look for 'the cause of the cause' and apply it to find solutions based on the panoramic view, rather than a snapshot of the problem. I learned how to balance it in a way that made sense to them, even though they came with a single idea of an issue with realizing the huge, detrimental downsides to it. The repercussions would be far too severe to get their issue solved because they had not considered all the ramifications of their solution, they were in effect treating a symptom.

When you look at your life at this point (and I looked at my life doing this), I thought, "What is the reality if I win this election? What's going to have to happen?" I would have to buy a house in Boise and live there part-time. The legislature meets three months out of the year. I would probably go to 12 to 14 meetings in between. I would be meeting people year-round. I would be paid little, and it would cost me $100,000 to actually be a legislator. Was I crazy? Yes. Did I think I could make a difference? Yes. Do I want to make a difference? I do. But when is the best timing to do that?

When we started, we felt very guided to do this and were very motivated. Shirley and I felt going forward was the right decision. Now, whether we won or not was a matter for God to decide. And the important thing was to go with what the Universe or God wanted us to do. When you go into a situation and look at what feels the best and is the "right" thing to do, if it feels good in your heart and the reasons why you're doing something are sound, you create a reality. What is the "tree" that I see going to look like? For me, the "tree" says that I go forward with running for office.

When I went into this election, I went in feeling a surprising amount of anxiety. I am quite used to putting myself out there, speaking and teaching professionals that often have a deep disregard for "chiropractors" and what they know. Standing in front of groups like that does not bother me a bit. Yet, suddenly putting myself out there for the masses was intimidating! Would

I win, would anyone vote for me? Would they dislike me? It forced me to take a long hard look at my self-worth and ask; "Can I take it that 40% of the people are probably going to hate me just for running, without even knowing me?" How will I deal with that and put it into perspective? I am going to make decisions that half the people probably aren't going to like. How does that fit into the paradigm of making sense? What are my reasons for running? Is it my ego? Is it someone else's ego? Is it to make me or another person happy? Is it to make money, gain fame, prestige? What really is the reason?

As the days leading up to the primary dwindled, I finally developed a sense of peace in my mind. Knowing I had done all I could do it was now a matter of waiting to see what God and the Universe had in store for me, preparing myself to take the next step. Signs appear that give clarity and purpose to your direction. We have talked before about this. Today I have lived my life to the fullest. I have done what I can do, and I am going to go to bed knowing tomorrow is going to be the next, best day of my life. Whatever happens is just how you frame that in your reality. What is your "tree" going to look like? Are there leaves on it or no leaves? Is it bear with 12 limbs or full of fruit? What is the perception of the reality of the "tree" you are looking at?

We have friends that have an election party every primary and main election night. We were there watching the results of the primary. There were people that evening that said, "Oh, I voted for you. I support you." Everybody was saying, "I hope you win." At about 10:30 the results started coming in, we were behind. I think at about 9:15, my stomach was up in my throat. We had to leave before the final numbers were in, finding out the results once we were home. I thought, wow, I lost by 6 percent. I was relieved. Due to the Covid virus, I had not been able to campaign. Considering I was running against an incumbent in a huge district in Idaho, I felt exceptionally good about how well I had done! I got my reality check.

People generally react without a clear understanding of the whole picture. Oftentimes we decide things based more on emotion or perception than on fact. We make decisions based on perceptions we have with a vested interest in what we want out of that reality. Is that an honest and realistic point? Probably not most of the time. Just being aware of that tendency can cause a reality shift. You see the "tree" now full of leaves. If you come from a restricted reality, your "tree" may have four limbs and no leaves, but you're comfortable with that and never push beyond your comfort zone.

When I went to bed the night of the primary, I lay there and mulled things over while my wife slept. Initially I felt this huge loss, an empty hollow feeling. It was a little bit rattling. I woke up the next morning and felt like I had lost my child or my pet. There was no dog to come and greet me that morning. I took my customary walk and cleared my head as I do daily. While I walked, I began to realize the hollow feeling was not disappointment as I'd initially thought, but rather the emptiness was the absence of stress and anxiety. Oh my gosh, this anchor that had been sitting on my shoulders the last four months had disappeared! I was no longer restrained by the reality I had created.

I have reached a point where I now have the freedom to take all the knowledge that I gained from that experience and send it in a direction that will accomplish more than my original thoughts. What an amazing, empowering feeling that was! But what I had to do is look at the fact that when you go through that door, when you see that "tree," we never know what it will look like until we get in the room. Until you have actually run for a position or take on a new job and look at what you think it is, compared to what it is in reality, and understand the realities, you cannot truly assess what it would be like.

I was able to assess the situation, open the door, have all the sensation, pressure and feeling of the experience without the consequence. "Wow, now that I understand what's in the room, I can walk back into it if I choose and understand the arrangement of the room." What a freeing feeling that is to know what it takes without having to be behind the eight-ball! I really was not ready to take it on completely. But now I can say I understand the reality of what it is, should I choose to walk into that room.

We know knowledge is power, and by knowing that, we can create the reality that makes the most sense for us. It was a blessing to go through what I went through. I learned so much and it allowed me to look at where everything else falls into place. Now, I am going to go forward armed with ideas I have been wanting to explore, goals I've wanted to accomplish. I understand how to go through the process in part from what I learned and from all the people I encountered and the experience I had in running for office.

In life, the lesson learned is that perceptions are how we choose to view things. Does the tree really need to move, or do we just need to go around it? The trick is learning to recognize that. Having the tree bear fruit or be barren is our choice My time running for office was an incredible eye-opener for me personally. It showed me that the realities we create by the experiences we have can easily be improved upon simply by choosing to do so. Every day can truly be the "best day" when we realize that situations happen, yet we control what impact they make on our reality. We must improve every day as to what we do. We must take every situation that happens, that gives us power and knowledge and use it to create a reality the next day that is better than the reality we had today.

Epilogue

"...the rest of the story."

—Paul Harvey

As of January 2020, we became acutely aware of the coronavirus or Covid-19 or the SARS evolution virus, the bat virus, or the China virus. What you call it seems to be based almost solely on your political affiliation as does the seriousness and fear generated by this pandemic. Never in my 40 years of practice have I witnessed anything that even compares to what is happening in the country today. But what is it really? With all the material that's been published on the internet, all of the ideas that have been posted, and all of the studies that have been done, we seem to be no closer to a consensus that we were in the beginning. I ask myself, how can that be? With the eyes of the entire world focused on this issue, we still have several vastly differing views. If we have factual information how can we still be so divided? The other disturbing thing I find is that what to do to slow, prevent, or combat the disease is also dependent on which theory you subscribe to. Everyone seems to subscribe to one reality or the other, with little factual information to substantiate their position. But let's talk about the actions that are happening.

In March 2020, Idaho shut down the entire state allowing only for necessary movement with stay at home legislation in place to shut the cities straight down. We reported 50 cases statewide. So, why did we shut it down? I looked at a study yesterday where 60% of the people were against shutting down, and 40% were for it. The governor—while I do not envy his position—was in a no-win situation either way. Why? Because of the need we've developed to be politically correct. Google defines *political correctness* as: "The avoidance, *often considered as taken to extremes*, of forms of expression or action that are *perceived* to exclude, marginalize, or insult groups of people who are socially disadvantaged or discriminated against." The word that jumps out at me is "perceived." So, it all goes back to perception, someone's perception. My first question is, Who's perception? My next is why do they get to decide how I perceive anything? Clearly, I'm not the only one who feels that way, as evidenced by the words, "often considered as taken to extremes" in the definition.

If we look at political correctness, I recall a conversation with my friend Keith, when he came up to visit in March. Being best friends growing up, we had many stories that we reminisced about. One story I recall was about a bicycle ride that ended with me being pitched over the handlebars and onto the pavement. I still vividly recall feeling my nose, knowing it was broken and bloody, a few tears as I looked back up 'dirt hill' which is the nickname of the hill above our street. As a 6-year-old it looked huge, but when I saw it a year ago it looked like a small bump. The point I wanted to make was this, in those days we never thought anything of those bumps and bruises, no one would have ever thought to wear a helmet when riding a bike! Today a child not wearing a helmet, is perceived as a sign of poor parenting.

I continually marvel at how things have changed over the years. Things that were done every day without thought, riding in the back of a pick-up truck, riding a bike without a helmet are today cause for being ostracized, and your parenting skills called into question, possibly even reported. The point is this, what is happening in our society to provoke these changes? How has our entire thought process changed and who is responsible for those changes? The who seem to be a ridiculously small group that has a very loud persistent voice. Hence the adage, "The squeaky wheel gets the grease."

The virus now is a classic example of a squeaky wheel getting the grease! What is the etiology of the disease? What is the etiology from a social point of view?

Our initial information was of the breakout of a mystery virus in China that acted like a strange pneumonia. We got the press on it. The press does what? It expands the story and tells us stories. Okay, now we have a story in the press that something is going on with a virus, but what is it? It is sensationalized with rumors and inuendoes of who started it, why it started, and if it's even real. Next is that it's coming to the US. What do we do? Our president—and it wouldn't have mattered who the president would have been—could never have taken the right action according to half the people in our country. You are wrong and you are right, no matter what action you choose. It was a no-win situation because we're so ingrained now that—and this is where the political correctness comes in —the government is here to save us. Someone needs to take care of this. And with that said, we see the country split in two. Half the people crying, "The government should take care of us!" And the other half crying, "We can take care of ourselves!"

Here now is the epitome of political correctness. If you do not wash your hands, if you do not wear a mask, if you do not quarantine all people, you're a bad person, you are selfish, and care only about yourself. If you wear a mask, half of the country thinks you're a hero and the other half thinks you've "drank the Kool-Aid." And if you don't wear a mask, you are despicable and selfish, perhaps even mentally diminished in some way and even worse, a conspiracy theorist! Take your pick, these seem to be the prevailing realities we can choose from. That is going to potentially do what? Possibly, someone will die. Are people going to die every day with or without this virus? YES. Are the numbers greater than or less than with this virus? We are still sorting those numbers out. It appears that because of politics, the numbers are being argued constantly. We really don't know, and probably we will never know with the games that are being played.

Now for the big question, where do we go from here? This book will be published in early 2021 and we still will not have answered this question. This question is at the bedrock of every decision we make going forward. We have reached a point where political correctness is absolutely controlling, defining, and shutting down our lives. It has paralyzed our nation, is destroying our economy, and creating a huge rift in our society. Forever changing our personal, social, emotional, and spiritual wellbeing by changing life as we knew it. How did we come to such a place in such a short amount of time? Who is responsible? George Soros, Bill Gates, Republicans, Democrats? What is the goal? More Government controls? Mandatory vaccinations, population control, promoting a globalist agenda? Take your pick, conspiracy theories abound!

The one thing that is certain is people will die whether from Covid, a car wreck, cancer, COPD or simply from old age—that is reality. After 40 years in practice I can tell you that is an absolute fact, it is one reality that doesn't change. What can change is how healthy you are until your time is up, this is something that you can control. Let's look at this a little more and ask where we go from here. Political correctness right now says that you need to quarantine yourself and keep away from people to keep from spreading the virus in order to keep people healthy. Let the government pay us to be off work. Let the government bail us out and tell us what to do next. Is that where we want to be 10 years from now? If this evolves the same amount in that timeframe, we will have a government that controls everything we do, tells us what to think, and dictates every facet of our daily lives. It takes away any ability for us to be in control of our lives. The biggest issue is to take responsibility for our lives. Political correctness has subverted our desire to be responsible for ourselves. That is the most impactful consequence of our current situation.

Today is the day to start anew. You need to know why this is important for yourself, and ultimately it will be better for everyone around you. I have been talking to doctors all over the world in the last six months. I spent time talking with a friend from Panama about how the virus was impacting them. Panama was totally shut down. The airport was closed. They had many people from all over the world come there who were infected. Panama has a huge expatriate population, so they naturally have a large influx of people from all over the world. These people were doomed right off the bat.

What was interesting to me was his theory of how the virus started. He is Chinese, born and raised in Panama, he presented me with many things that indicated the whole thing came from the US Military conducting military exercises in China. I shared one source of information asserting that the virus came out of a lab in North Carolina, was transferred to a lab in Wuhan, China, which was connected to Bill Gates. They were attempting to build a universal viral vaccination and the virus got out of that lab. The Chinese lab was reportedly funded by the US. It seems apparent the virus was manufactured and mutated by scientists. I have read dozens of articles that this virus could never have naturally mutated from a bat. The truth will likely never be public knowledge.

The AIDS virus is a good example of a dismal failure to find a vaccine, despite millions of dollars spent. Look at the success we've had with the flu vaccine. It appears virtually impossible to manufacture a vaccination. It makes me wonder how they think they can create an effective vaccine for the Covid virus.

When the Ebola virus broke out from 2013 to 2016 in Sierra Leone, mortality rates were upwards of 40 to 60%. A friend of mine, Dr. R., was very enthusiastic to go and treat people in Africa in 2015. He called and received permission from the government to go in the Fall of 2015. His treatment was ozone and silver, and he called me to discuss procedures and protocols. I helped him to get lined up and he headed to Africa. He arrived in late December 2015. His experience was treating six different people who improved in two or three days using direct IV ozone (because they didn't have the equipment or supplies to do anything more complicated). By the fifth day he was there, he was told by the President of Sierra Leone, "Either you treat my family exclusively or leave the country." His life was in danger and he left the country within six days of arriving. He was monitored by our health system in the US for a month afterwards. In January 2016, officials came to a seminar that he was presenting at and checked his temperature in front of all the attendees. It was quite dramatic!

In April of 2016 Dr. R. spoke at an orthomolecular medicine seminar I was attending in San Francisco. Dr. R. told the story of how he healed people with ozone. The next speaker was a forensic virologist. He also had traveled to Sierra Leone. He explained certain protein markers are often used to indicate a viral process in a person's blood. These markers are not exclusive to Ebola or any other specific disease, but their presence may indicate a viral process. He said that the people tested had these protein markers. The World Health Organization declared it to be Ebola, yet the actual virus was never specifically found. In mid-February, the WHO gave Sierra Leone about half a billion dollars. The previous six months, WHO was giving $40,000 per deceased person to the government of Sierra Leone to bury the bodies and contain the virus. Within two weeks (the middle of February 2016), the Sierra Leone government received the half-billion dollars, and the Ebola virus magically disappeared.

The pathologist said that Ebola was purely engineered. They could mimic the markers of Ebola, but there was never any actual Ebola virus found. It was more likely a neurotoxin or a poison gas of some sort that killed the people there. This makes the most sense, as ozone is great at treating mustard gas exposure and things of that nature, however it is not capable of killing a virus in the blood. It kills virus and bacteria on *direct contact* only. So, was the Ebola scare truth or fiction? I have a presentation model from the US Department of Defense going back 10 years showing how Ebola can be stopped using colloidal silver products. The Ebola virus is easy to destroy. If you remember the doctor that "contracted Ebola" and was brought back to the US from Africa in 2015. Despite heavy doses of antiviral medication, he died. The antiviral meds had no effect on the "virus." The question is, was it really the Ebola virus? We may never know because they buried the results (meaning, all of the people affected).

As a side note, I got a business card from the virologist that spoke that day, being very intrigued by his story. I tried to reach him about a month after the conference. I never was able to contact him, he just disappeared. I can't help but wonder what happened. That really sounds like a conspiracy theory, but it's what happened.

Now look at the Covid-19 virus as of October 1, 2020. We now know it has an S-protein attached to it, which is not naturally occurring. This means the immune system responds differently to it causing a different immune response, so people can be at higher risk. It has come out in studies that almost 30% of the people in the country have a natural immunity to the virus. Part of the reason is that the basic coronavirus has been around for years. We also see that higher areas of death rates are concurrent with higher risk patient's that have comorbidities. We see that areas that have 5G seem to have a higher death rate. On the other hand, countries such as France and Iran who do not have 5G, are seeing their rates rise again.

Another factor may be high levels of immunizations seemingly related to higher death rates. It appears that vaccinations interfere with the body's natural immune response. The virus is not recognized by the immune systems, allowing it to attack cell walls and cause a cytokine storm. We see younger people with stronger T-cells, which are the antiviral elements in the blood that affect the immune system having a much lower risk level. We also find the virus rapidly mutates upwards of 30 times in a year. It seems pointless to manufacture a vaccination for something that continues to mutate. This begs the question, what is the why of the why?

There are treatment options using steroids, antibiotics, as well as natural methods that have been extremely effective in treating this virus upon onset. When we add money into the equation is where things go south on us. Medicare pays hospitals $13,000 for each Covid-19 diagnosis. We also see that if they use ventilators, they get $35,000. The mortality rate of people placed on ventilators is 85%, but using a ventilator is the standard of care, the fact it kills people is acceptable. I addressed this concept earlier in the book.

There are numerous studies of everything from ozone to blood therapies that boost the immune system. Many are extremely easy to administer, cost effective, and are effective treatment options. Unfortunately, the drug companies do not make any money from it so we will never see that in mainstream medicine. We really need to follow the money. To date the press has avoided that, Facebook, and Google censor anything outside mainstream medical treatment. Instead, they downplay every alternative treatment as bogus. I have talked to almost 50 doctors around the country that have successfully treated Covid with no deaths. I had a conversation with the doctor today who is using one dose of 25g of Vitamin C IV, completely curing people with this illness in the Southern California area.

I want to make a prediction. This part of the book was written at the end of September 2020. I predict studies will show that cloth masks are totally worthless, and if not worthless, they are causing more problems. Today there are no studies showing cloth masks work in a group setting. I will also predict that this virus will not go away with the election in November 2020.

The end game for the pandemic will force mandatory vaccination with chips of some sort to monitor when you have had your vaccination. That will force you to have a chip to travel, work, buy food, go to the bank, and live. There is a large push for artificial intelligence. This has to be connected. I checked on several sites and there are 40,000 satellites set to be launched in the next five years, all tied into artificial intelligence and tracking. My wife and I watched a series of 23 satellites on the same trajectory 15 seconds apart twice now in the last six months. We sit out every night and look at the sky from the hot tub. I have had other people report seeing the same thing.

This topic is another book. You can debate the last several paragraphs. All I ask is that YOU THINK FOR YOURSELF. The takeaway of this chapter is to empower you with the ability to choose. You can choose left or right. The future is your destination, now YOU make the choice. It is your turn to think and solve.

I know some of you may think I'm pushing the envelope with what I just said. Mark my words, those ideas are already on someone's drawing board. The future will be whatever we let happen. It's time for us to decide. Become involved, be educated, and be vocal. Silence is not our friend right now. Will you see the tree as you want it to be, or will you let someone else decide what the tree looks like?

About the Author

Dr. Dennis L. Harper

With 40 years in practice, Dr. Dennis Harper is just reaching a point where he feels he knows enough to treat people! He says this because he is finally able to take a lifetime of accumulated knowledge and apply it to a vast array of increasingly sick individuals. Many people present with complex, diverse symptoms that can easily confuse and trick us into treating symptoms, often obscuring the underlying problem. Dr. Harper was fortunate to receive a superior foundational education at Western States Chiropractic College and continued to study over the years with Dr. John Brimhall, Dr. Klinghart, Dr. Frank Shallenberger, Dr. Robert Rowan, and others in the Alternative Medical field. This has led him to inquire always, "What is the cause of the cause," continually looking one step beyond the present. Speaking nationally and training practitioners for many years have honed his diagnostic skills and the ability to listen to a patient's body rather than their words.

Printed in the USA
CPSIA information can be obtained
at www.ICGtesting.com
LVHW021627311223
767596LV00011B/73